'A KIND OF BIBLE'

Vincent van Gogh as Evangelist

Anton Wessels

D1423701

SCM PRESS

Translated by John Bowden from the Dutch *'Een Soort Bijbel.' Vincent van Gogh als evangelist*, published 1990 by Uitgevereij Ten Have b.v., Baarn, The Netherlands, with additional material supplied by the author, 2000.

© Uitgeverij Ten Have b.v., Baarn 1990, 2000

Translation © John Bowden 2000

All rights reserved. No part of this publication may be reproduced, stored in a retrieval system, or transmitted, in any form or by any means, electronic, mechanical, photocopying or otherwise, without the prior permission of the publisher, SCM Press.

SCM Press wishes to express its deep gratitude to the Van Coeverden-Adriani Stichting for a grant towards the cost of translation, which made the publication of this book possible

0 334 02805 1

This edition first published 2000 by
SCM Press
9–17 St Albans Place London N1 0NX

SCM Press is a division of
SCM-Canterbury Press Ltd

Printed in Great Britain by
Biddles Ltd, Guildford and King's Lynn

To the memory of my wife Toke,
and her father and mother,
a family from Van Gogh's Brabant

Contents

Introduction

'And my own future is a cup that will not pass me by unless I drink it. So "Fiat voluntas".'

(The Hague, 313)

To begin with, Vincent van Gogh wanted to become a preacher. For a short time he was an assistant preacher in England. But his efforts to be accepted for regular preacher's training in Amsterdam failed. He came to grief over the admission requirements for theological study, in particular a knowledge of the classical languages, Latin and above all Greek. On the advice of his father he then trained in Brussels to become an evangelist. However, he succeeded in working as an evangelist *only* (!) in the Borinage, a mining district in Belgium. There he discovered his vocation as a painter.

Many people have interpreted this move not only as the abandonment of the ideal to become a preacher but also as a break with Christian religion and faith. His 'conversion' from evangelist to painter is said to have meant an abandonment of the Christian faith.

In this book I want above all to show that Vincent van Gogh was not only a preacher and evangelist for a few years but that even in following his vocation as a painter he remained an evangelist.

Emotion

Anyone who gets involved with Vincent van Gogh cannot help being moved, moved at this man who in his short life – like the painters Raphael and Caravaggio he did not live to be more than thirty-seven – suffered much and found little recognition either as an evangelist or as a painter.

Today Vincent van Gogh is a world-famous painter and countless people know his works through the originals and/or reproductions. Vincent himself would have been glad about the reproductions, because he wanted works of art to be accessible to a wide public. Speaking about lithographs he wrote: 'No result of my work could please me better than for ordinary working people to hang such prints (almshouse man) in their room or workshop. I think what Herkomer said, It is really done for you – the public, is true' (245: for the references to the letters cf. the explanation in the bibliography).

Letters

Vincent van Gogh left not only drawings and paintings but also numerous letters. In a moving way they help us to share in the course of his life. This is above all true of the letters to his brother Theo, his 'comrade', to use Theo's own words. These human documents of inestimable value 'make us privy,' as George Steiner writes, 'to the mystery' of this man (Steiner, 17). The letters of a man who was once rejected as an evangelist because he did not have 'the gift of the word' (143a) are as moving and exciting to read as if they had been written yesterday. Karl Jaspers, who in a book about Strindberg and Van Gogh points out the difference in the letters before and after 1880, notes the deep seriousness in all the letters before and during the psychosis – during the last two years of Van Gogh's life: 'These letters (and only around a quarter of them come from the time of the psychosis) in their totality are the documentation of a world-view, an existence, a lofty ethos, the expression of an unconditional truthfulness, a deeply irrational faith, an infinite love, a generous humanity, an unshaken *amor fati*. They have been counted among the most compelling to have appeared in the most recent past' (Jaspers, 154).

How vivid his language was may be seen, for example, from a letter in which he discusses ambition and love.

'My opinion is that when it develops, when it comes to its full development, love produces better characters than the opposite passion: Ambition & Co. But just because love is so strong, generally in our youth (I mean at seventeen, eighteen or twenty) we are usually not strong enough to keep going straight. The passions are the little ship's sails, you see, and anyone who gives way entirely to his feelings in his twentieth year catches too much wind and his boat takes in too much water and he sinks, or comes to the surface again after all. By contrast, anyone who hoists the sail of Ambition & Co. and no other on his mast sails through life on a straight course without accidents, without wavering until finally, finally, finally, circumstances arise which make him think, 'I haven't enough sail.' Then he says, 'I would give everything I possess for one square metre of sail, and I do not have it.' He becomes desperate. And now he remembers that he can add another power; he thinks of the sail which he has despised until now, which he had put away with the ballast. And it is this sail that saves him. Love's sail must save him; without hoisting it, he cannot arrive' (157, Etten, 12 November 1881).

Lack of money

All his life Vincent had to contend with a lack of money. Though in The Hague he could write that he was not often 'rich in money', 'but (though it doesn't happen every day) rich – because I have found in my work something to which I can devote myself heart and soul, which inspires me and gives a meaning to life' (274), he was all too aware of his lack of success in the financial sense of the word. He knew that he was a 'poor painter' and that he faced 'yet more years of struggle'. He felt compelled to live his life 'rather like a farm labourer or a factory hand does' (313).

It was above all his brother Theo whom put him in a financial position to go on painting. In the letters Theo is often thanked for having sent money or sometimes blamed for being a day or two late.

Vincent was aware that the kind of work that he produced was not particularly saleable. He touched on this question several times: 'As you – Theo – will remember, when you were here, you said that some day I should try to send you a little drawing of a "saleable" nature. However, you must excuse my not knowing precisely when a drawing is of that kind and when it is not. I used to think I knew, but now I see day by day that I'm mistaken. However, I hope that this little bench (which he had drawn), if not yet saleable, will show you that I am not averse sometimes to choosing subjects which are pleasant or attractive, and as such seem more likely to find buyers than things of a more gloomy nature' (230). Clearly Theo had written to Vincent a couple of times that his work was 'almost saleable . . .' (358)

During his life Vincent was able to sell only one of his paintings – 'The Red Vineyard', which brought in 400 francs (200 guilders).

He repeatedly spoke of the cost of the paintings, which was not covered by the sale. 'Don't I deserve my bread if I work hard? Or am I not worth the means which enable me to work?', he asked himself in The Hague (183). In the summer of 1887 he writes from Paris: 'It depresses me to think that even when it's a success, painting never pays back what it costs' (462). In Arles he sighed: 'But I dare to hope that one day we'll get back some of the money that we spend, and if I had more money, I should spend even more on trying to produce very rich and colourful canvases' (508). 'It's a gloomy enough prospect to say that perhaps the paintings I'm doing will have some value. If they were worth their cost, then I could tell myself, "I never bothered my head about money"' (524). Vincent was always oppressed by this lack of money. 'But the money that it costs to paint crushes me with a feeling of guilt and worthlessness and it would be a good thing, if possible, for this to stop' (589).

Among other things, the mania for work which drove Vincent had to do with anxiety about money: 'Oh, if only every artist had enough to live on, and to work on! But as that is not the case, I want to produce, to produce a lot, devoting all my energy to it' (542). 'Precisely because in the end of the day there is no way in which I can ever cover the costs, I feel the need to produce even to the extent that I am mentally crushed and physically drained as a result. I can't help it that my paintings don't sell. Nevertheless the day will come when people will see that they are worth more than the cost of the paint and my own extremely meagre upkeep that we put into them' (557).

That day has indeed come, but not during Vincent's lifetime. It is terrible to have to note that now in our time, a century after his death, as his paintings come up for sale, they vie with one another for record prices, going well into the tens of millions of dollars. Even letters of his which are not particularly special produce vast sums of money.

'A kind of Bible'

At the time of an exhibition in the Van Gogh Museum in Amsterdam in 1988, 'Hard Times, Social Themes in Victorian Art 1849–1900', a survey was given of Van Gogh's art, often through reproductions in journals like *The Graphic* or *The Illustrated London News*. At one time Vincent owned twenty-one volumes of *The Graphic*, covering the years 1870–1880 (R 22). Hubert von Herkomer (1849–1913) was one of Vincent's favourite artists. This English painter, engraver and sculptor, of German origin, worked for *The Graphic* in London from 1870.

On this occasion another exhibition was arranged in the print cabinets, 'A Kind of Bible', comprising the collections which Vincent van Gogh had made of illustrations from

French, American, German, Dutch and above all English journals. From these illustrations he derived ideas for his own work. As he himself said, their work was 'a kind of Bible' for him (Van Tilborgh, 1981, 1, 119). 'A collection of prints like these becomes, in my opinion, a kind of Bible to an artist, in which he reads now and then to put himself in the mood' (R 25).

Plan

The plan of this book is as follows. After a sketch of Vincent Van Gogh's life and work in Chapter 1, there is an account of his attempt to become a preacher like his father, whom he admired very much, and the degree to which he became one, above all in England and Belgium. For a short time he was an evangelist (Chapter 2). Thirdly, with reference to some of his works of art and letters, I shall demonstrate how in a sense he also remained a preacher and evangelist, though in the style of an artist (Chapter 3). Chapter 4 investigates 'Van Gogh's Christ'. The last chapter shows how Vincent van Gogh as an evangelist/painter wanted to bring comfort and above all light. Van Gogh's drawings and paintings can be seen as a 'kind of Bible'.

Epiphany 1990

A Sketch of Vincent's Life and Works

'Thy way, not mine, O Lord,
however dark it be,
Lead me by thine own hand
Choose out the path for me.'

(One of the hymns which Vincent thought were 'beautiful',
quoted in a letter from Paris, 41)

His youth

Vincent Willem van Gogh was born on 30 March 1853 at Groot Zundert in the province of North Brabant. He was the oldest son of a Dutch Reformed preacher Theodorus van Gogh (1822–1885) and Anna Cornelia Carbentus (1819–1907). There were many preachers in his family, like Dr J. P. Stricker in Amsterdam, who was married to his mother's sister Wilhelmina Catrina Gerarda Carbentus. His grandfather Vincent van Gogh (1789–1874) was a preacher in Breda from 1822. Among his forefathers was a Van Gogh who was a Remonstrant preacher in Boskoop.

Before Vincent's birth his parents had a stillborn child who bore the same name – Vincent Willem. It has often been said that Vincent van Gogh's life was also marked by this fact. He regularly went past a grave with his own name on it. On the tombstone lying next to the church he would read:

Vincent van Gogh 1852
Let the little children come to me
For of such is the kingdom of God
Luke 18.16.

In the Zundert register he has the same number, 29, as his dead brother (Tralbaut, 1966, 79,10).

His brother Theo was born four years later, in 1857. In a letter to Theo, Theodorus Van Gogh compares his two sons to Jacob and Esau. Vincent is Esau (Edwards, 8).

The minister's children were not allowed to play in the street. Every day they went for a one-hour walk under the protection of their parents and governess. The parents projected on to the children their own vulnerability, which was the consequence of having the children. Vincent's father was described as 'an apostle of fashion' (Meyers, 51).

Theo was to play a crucial role in Vincent's life. Vincent had a special relationship with him. His unique correspondence bears witness to this. The two corresponded from the time when Vincent was nineteen – August 1872. 'I have no real friend but you, and when I feel emotional, you are always in my thoughts,' he wrote from The Hague on 22 July 1883 (302). '*You do know that I think that you've saved my life*, and I *shall never* forget it; *though we put an end* to relations which I fear would bring us into a wrong relationship, I am not only your brother, your friend, but at the same time I have *infinite* obligations of gratitude to you for lending me a helping hand at the time, and continuing to help me. Money can be paid back, but not friendship like yours' (Nüenen, 346).

After first going to a boarding school in Zevenbergen, where among other things he was well taught in French, in September Vincent went to the High School in Tilburg. There he spent another two years, until March 1868.

Six years in the art business

There were not only preachers but also various art dealers in Vincent's family: Uncle Hein, first in Rotterdam and then in Brussels; Uncle Cor in Amsterdam; and Uncle Vincent in The Hague. Uncle Vincent merged with Goupil and Co, which had branches in The Hague, London, Brussels and Paris. Vincent van Gogh found his first employment in this branch of work. In July 1869 he became the youngest employee in the family art business of Goupil and Co in the 'Plaats' in The Hague (1869–1873). From this branch he was sent with good references to London – May 1873 to May 1875 (with a break in Paris between October and December 1874). In May 1875, at the request of his parents he was transferred to the Goupil head office in Paris (May 1875–1 April 1877).

To begin with, Vincent was happy in his work. From London he wrote on 9 February 1874 to Mrs Caroline van Stockum-Haanebeek: 'I live a rich life here, "having nothing yet possessing all things", I am sometimes inclined to believe that I'm gradually turning into a cosmopolitan; that is, neither a Dutchman, an Englishman or a Frenchman but simply a man' (13a).

In London – in 1873 – he fell in love with the daughter of his host, Eugénie Loyer, the daughter of the widow Loyer. He asked for her hand, but she refused him. Vincent was not aware that she was already engaged. It was Vincent's first love. This rejection led to a crisis for him. He left London and returned to Paris.

But he increasingly turned against this trade, in which business and not art was central. In this period he read a great deal. In his free time he devoted a good deal of time to Bible reading, which was a great comfort to him.

In a letter of 8 May 1875 from London he enclosed a quotation from Renan: 'To act in the world one must die to oneself. The person aware of being a missionary of a religious thought has no other homeland than this thought.'

However, in 1876 he was dismissed from the art trade.

Teacher/evangelist/preacher

Back in England, Vincent first worked as a teacher and gave French lessons in Ramsgate. Mr William Port Stokes ran a private boarding school there where Vincent worked for a

month. In June 1876 the school was moved to Isleworth, on
the Thames to the south-west of London. Mr Stokes asked
him among other things to collect school fees in the poorest
districts of London. In July 1876 Vincent moved to a school
run by Thomas Slade Jones (1829–1883) and became a
Methodist (auxiliary) preacher; for nine months (April–
December) he worked as an evangelist.

From Isleworth, on 17 November 1876, among other
things Vincent wrote: 'While I sit writing to you in my little
room and it's so very, very quiet, I look at your portraits and
the prints on the wall – "*Christus Consolator*", "Good
Friday", "Women Visiting the Tomb", "The Old Huguenot",
Ary Scheffer's "The Prodigal Son", "A Little Boat on a Stormy
Sea" . . . and when I think of you all and everything here . . .
then I feel, Hear, Lord, the prayer that my mother said for me
when I left home – and on Good Friday at that!' (62).
'"Father, I pray you that you do not take him out of the world,
but that you preserve him from evil", and "Lord, make me my
father's brother, a Christian and a Christian worker, complete
your work that you have begun in me"' (81).

That Vincent steeped himself so intensively in religious
reading is also evident from his letters. Of course his parents
could not disapprove, but the fanaticism which he displayed
went too far for them. 'Oh, if only he would simply learn to be
a child and not get so excited, and worked up over biblical
texts,' wrote his father to Theo on 8 September 1876. 'The
more it goes on, the more it worries us and I fear that one day
he will become unsuited to practical life. It's a bitter, bitter
shame' (Hulsker, *Close-up*, 73). In one of her letters to Theo,
his sister Lies called him a 'church maniac' (ibid., 74).

Vincent does not say in his letter precisely what or who
made him to go back to the Netherlands (83) – himself or his
parents or both? On his return there, he worked for a couple
of months – from 21 January to 30 April 1877 – as a trainee/
errand boy in a bookshop in Dordrecht.

In May of the same year, however, he moved to Amsterdam, where he lived in a little room in the dockyard of his Uncle Johan (Jan). In Amsterdam he wanted to try for admission to theological training with a view to becoming a real preacher. For a while he had lessons from Mendes da Costa, who attempted to teach him Latin and Greek.

However, Vincent did not succeed in passing his state examination. In July 1878 he gave up his studies and for a few months took a training course for evangelists in Brussels. At the end of this the mission committee refused to give him an appointment as evangelist, at least initially. But Vincent did go as an evangelist to the Belgian mining district of the Borinage from 1878 to 1880. In January 1878, to his great joy an official appointment followed. He lived in the mining area and shared the miners' life of poverty. He did this work until he was dismissed in 1880.

Vincent's father had planned to have his oldest son committed to a mental institution, in the Belgian village of Gheel near Antwerp. 'The Gheel business of last year, when Pa wanted to put me in an asylum!' (Letters 159, cf. 198, 204, 212, 216; Hulsker, 12, 127)

Vocation as an artist

After the end of his involvement as an evangelist in July 1879, Vincent in fact spent many months drawing. After he had overcome the disappointment of his dismissal, art becomes the main, almost the only, subject of Vincent's letters to Theo until he left the Borinage for good. Thus his career as an artist began in July 1879 (Hulsker, *Close-up*, 126). In a long letter to Theo from July 1880 there is much that sheds light on this change in the direction of his life. He examines himself and gives a reason for this self-examination: 'It's true that occasionally I've earned my crust of bread, occasionally a friend has given it to me in charity. I've lived as I could, as luck would have it. It's true that I have lost the confidence of various people; it's true that my financial affairs are in a sorry state;

it's true that the future is just as gloomy; it's true that I might
have done better; it's true that I've lost time in terms of earning my living; it's true that my studies are in a rather depress-
ing and hopeless condition, and that my failings are greater –
infinitely greater – than my achievements. But is that "going
downhill"? Is that "doing nothing"? You will perhaps say,
"But why didn't you continue as they wanted you to, and go
to the university?" My only answer is that it cost too much
and besides, that future was not much better than the one
which I now face. But I must continue on the path I've taken.
If I don't do anything, if I don't study, if I don't go on seeking
any longer, I am lost. Then woe is me. That's how I look at it:
what is necessary is to keep going on. But you will ask, "What
is your definite aim?" That aim becomes more definite, will
stand out slowly and surely, as the rough draft becomes a
sketch and the sketch a picture – little by little, by working
seriously on it, by pondering on the first vague idea, the first
fleeting and passing thought, so as to fix it. You should know
that with evangelists it's the same as with artists' (133).

Almost two years later he said about this move that had
he been competent to be a minister or a dealer in the work of
others, 'then perhaps I shouldn't have been fit for drawing and
painting and should neither have resigned nor accepted my
dismissal as such' (The Hague, 15/27 April 1882, 190).
However, Vincent's way to becoming an artist – he first
concentrated on the study of drawing, in which he tried to
reproduced reality (141) – did not go easily. While still in
Belgium he wrote:

'. . .Well, even in the depths of misery I felt my energy revive
and I said to myself, Despite everything, I shall get over it. I
shall set to work with my pencil, which I had thrown away in
my deep dejection, and draw again. From that moment everything seems to have changed for me . . . Just wait, perhaps
you'll see that I too am a worker. Though I can't predict what
I shall be able to do . . .' (Cuesmes, 24 September 1880, 136).

Vincent even once doubted this vocation. On 22 July 1883

he wrote from The Hague: 'Now I thought, I'm sorry that I didn't fall ill and die in the Borinage at that time, instead of painting. For I'm only a burden to you' (302). In the last years of his life – in Arles in 1888 – when he was tormented with sickness, he still kept thinking about this vocation: 'Oh, it seems to me more and more that *people* are the root of every-thing, and though it will always be a melancholy thought that one is not part of real life, in the sense that it's more worth while to work in flesh and blood itself than in paint or plaster, more worth while to produce children than paintings or engage in business, all the same you feel that you're alive when you remember that you have friends among these who are just as much outside real life as you are' (476). A month later he wrote: 'In the midst of an artist's life there is, and remains, and always comes back at particular moments, the nostalgia for the ideal life, which can never be realized. And sometimes one lacks all the desire to throw oneself heart and soul into art and to get well again for that' (489).

It had been Vincent's brother Theo who suggested to him that he should choose this career as a painter. In the period between 1880 and his death in 1890 it was Theo who made it financially possible for him.

In Brussels, to which he moved initially, he applied himself to drawing. Theo put him in contact with the painter Anthon Gerard van Rappard (1858–1892), with whom Vincent con-tinued to correspond for five years.

Etten

From April 1881 Vincent again lived with his parents, who had meanwhile moved from Zundert to Etten, also in Brabant. In the meantime Vincent's father had become preacher there. Vincent stayed in Etten from April to Dec-ember 1881. He continued above all to study drawing.

In Etten Vincent met his second 'great love'. He fell in love with his cousin Kee Vos. Her full name was Cornelia Adriana

Stricker (1846–1918). She was the daughter of Vincent's uncle the Revd Mr Stricker. In 1872 she was married to Dr Christoffel Martinus Vos. Vos had been preacher in Heenvliet, but had had to resign this office because of a serious chronic illness. In Amsterdam Vincent visited her regularly: 'I spent Monday evening with Vos and Kee; they love each other truly, and one can see that where love dwells, the Lord commands his blessing. It is a nice home, but it's a pity that he could not remain a preacher' (110). In 1878 Vos died, and Kee was left a widow with one child.

However, Kee resolutely rejected Vincent's offer of marriage: 'To her, past and future remain one, and so she can never return my feelings,' wrote Vincent to Theo (153). But Vincent could not rest content with this refusal. However, his appearance led to domestic difficulties between Vincent and his parents, especially his father. 'Now that causes me much sorrow and suffering, *but* I cannot believe that a father who cursed his son and (think of the past year) wanted to send him to a madhouse (which of course I resist with all my strength), calling the love of his son "untimely and unchaste", will work out right' (158). Vincent wanted to persuade Kee, who had meanwhile left Etten and moved to Amsterdam, to change her mind. 'Old chap,' he wrote to Theo, 'I must see her face again and speak to her once more. If I don't do it soon then perhaps something will happen at the great festival which would do me much harm. Don't ask me to say precisely what. If you were in love, too, you would understand; because you aren't in love I can't make things clear to you. Now, Theo, I need the fare to travel to Amsterdam' (157).

Vincent indeed travelled to Amsterdam with the thought that 'her "no, no, never", was not strong enough to make me give her up. I still had hope' (193). However, this attempt ended in total failure. Kee Vos did not even want to see Vincent again. Later he wrote about this painful experience in The Hague: 'You know I believe in God, I did not doubt the power of love, but then I felt something of "My God, my God, why have you forsaken me?", and everything went blank. I thought, Have I been deceiving myself? . . . "O God, there is no God." That terrible cold reception in Amsterdam was too much for me; my eyes were opened at last. Enough' (193).

His disappointment over the rejection of his approach and his behaviour alienated Vincent from his own milieu: 'You see, Theo, I am tired and weary . . . Knowing the prejudices of the world I realize that there is nothing for me to do but withdraw from the circle of my class, which of course has already long cast me out' (193).

The Hague

In December 1881, Vincent moved to The Hague, where he was to remain until September 1883. There he studied with his nephew Anton Mauve (1838–1888), a well-known painter. Mauve was a self-made man. Vincent asked and received from him support and advice for his own development as a painter. He wrote about his work and its character in The Hague. 'Whether in figure or in landscape, I would want to express not something sentimental and melancholy, but serious pain. In short, I want to make people say of my work: that man feels deeply, and that man has sensitive feelings. Despite my so-called roughness, you understand, perhaps precisely because of that . . . Supposing that everything were precisely so, then I would want to show through my work what there is in the heart of such an eccentric, of such a nobody' (218).

Van Gogh's first original works were produced in his period in The Hague. They comprise drawings of both people and landscapes.

Living with Sien

In The Hague, at the end of January 1882 or perhaps earlier, Vincent met Sien, a prostitute. Her full name was Clasina Maria Hoornik (1850–1904), called Christine or usually Sien.

When he got to know her she was an unmarried mother, expecting her second child, and on the bottle. Also influenced by his disappointing experiences in Amsterdam, Vincent was attracted by her fate (198). Of the motivation to take her he wrote: 'Last winter I met a pregnant woman, abandoned by the man whose child she bore in her body. A pregnant woman walking the streets in the winter has to earn her bread, you know how. I took this woman as a model and have worked with her all the winter. I couldn't pay her the full wages of a model, but that didn't prevent my paying her rent, and so far, thank God, I've been able to protect her and her child from hunger and cold, by sharing my own bread with her. When I met this woman, she attracted my attention because she looked ill' (192). Vincent began to live with her.

It is clear from his letters how he was thought of by those around him and what Vincent himself thought: 'Oh, there's gossip enough because I'm always in her company, but why should that bother me? I've never had such a good assistant as this ugly?? faded woman. To me she's beautiful, and I find in her exactly what I need; her life has been rough, and pain and adversity have marked her – now I can do something with her. If the ground has not been ploughed, you can get nothing from it. She has been ploughed – so I find more in her than in a crowd of unploughed ones' (R 8).

Vincent would not be put off his relationship with her. 'The way things stand with Sien is that I'm really attached to her and she to me; she's a faithful helper, who goes everywhere with me and who is becoming more indispensable to me day by day.' 'She and I are two unhappy people who keep each other company and share our burdens, and that is precisely why unhappiness is giving place to happiness, and the unbearable is becoming bearable. Now you will understand that, provided I remained faithful to her, I should set little store by the formality of marriage if the family didn't. Pa for one, and I know this for certain, attaches great importance to it, and although he won't approve of my marrying her, he would consider it even worse if I lived with her without marrying her' (204).

The 'liaison' between Vincent and Sien lasted for twenty months. Vincent's departure was not only connected with the fact that life with Sien had become impossible, but also because Vincent was convinced that he could live and work more cheaply in the country (Hulsker, *Close-up*, 54).

Drenthe

From September 1883 to November 1885 Vincent stayed in Drenthe. There he painted a number of sombre dark-brown landscapes.

These months in Drenthe were certainly not very easy. As later in Brabant, people around him gave him rather strange looks: 'I say loneliness and not solitude, that loneliness which a painter has to bear whom everyone in some isolated area regards as a lunatic, a murderer, a tramp, etc.' (343).

Painting peasants in Brabant

After the months in Drenthe Vincent again returned to his parents in Brabant for a while – from December 1883 to November 1885. His father had meanwhile become a preacher in Nuenen in a predominantly (98%) Roman Catholic area. He was aware that his parent regarded him as a 'shaggy dog' who keeps coming into the room with his 'wet paws' (346). He wrote in Nuenen: 'In the daytime, in ordinary life, I may sometimes look as thick-skinned as a wild boar, and I can well understand that people think me *coarse*' (6/7 December 1883, 345). 'I tell you, I deliberately chose the dog's path . . . I will remain a dog. I shall become poor, I shall become a painter, I want to remain human – going into nature' (around 17 December 1883, Nuenen, 347). Vincent spoke of himself as rough in connection with his alienation from his parental home (Edwards, 10).

There was no lack of difficulties with his parents in this period, although time and again there was a degree of understanding. 'I'm softened in my opinion, also because I seem to detect in Pa proof (and one of your hints fits in with this to a certain extent) that he really can't follow me when I try to explain something to him' (347). But alienation developed in Nuenen. This was again connected with a love drama, this time with Margot Begemann, who fell in love with Vincent. The Begemann family lived next door to the manse in Nuenen. Margot Begemann was twelve years older than Vincent. Compassion for a fellow human being played a role in the contact with her. 'Theo, I feel such damned pity for this woman, just because her age, and perhaps a disease of the liver and gall-bladder, menace her so terribly' (378). Her suicide attempt caused some commotion: 'Margot Begemann took poison in a moment of despair; after she had had a discussion with her family and they slandered her and me, she became so upset that she did it (in a moment of decided mania, I think)' (375).

On 26 March 1885 Vincent's father suddenly died of a heart attack on the threshold of his own home. On 30 March 1885 he was buried in the churchyard near the tower which Vincent often painted and which was later demolished. The tombstone still recalls the last resting place of this pastor and teacher of Nuenen from 1882 to 1885 (Brouwer, 70).

Vincent van Gogh worked for a while in Nuenen in a studio which was hired from a Roman Catholic sexton. However, the local Roman Catholic pastor in Nuenen forbade his parishioners to be models for Vincent. This was connected with the rumours that Gordina de Groot, who was to be immortalized in 'The Potato Eaters', was expecting a child by him (Tralbaut, 1966, 95; Nater, 142). The only thing that Vincent says about this is: 'These last two weeks I've had a great deal of trouble from the Roman Catholic pastors, who told me . . . that I oughtn't to get too familiar with people below my rank; those who spoke to me in such terms used quite a different tone towards the "people of lower rank", threatening them about having themselves painted by me . . . The priest even went so far as to promise people money if they refused to be painted; however, the people retorted quite spiritedly that they would rather earn money from me than beg some from him' (423).

Vincent got the nickname 'the little painter fellow' in the area (433). It was his aspiration to become a 'peasant-painter'. He depicted weavers and farmers in quite dark colours: 'When I call myself a peasant-painter, that really is the case . . . It is not in vain that I have spent so many evenings in the homes of the miners, and peat-cutters, and weavers, and farmers, musing by the fire, unless I was too hard at work for musing' (400). Much later he writes to his mother that he now sees himself as a peasant from Zundert: 'Well, I am ploughing on my canvas as they – the peasants – do on their fields' (612).

The period in Nuenen, North Brabant, has been called Vincent van Gogh's most important Dutch period of painting. Among the paintings from this Brabant period is his most famous painting. 'The Potato Eaters'. Of this work he says later in a letter, in the second half of 1887, to his sister Wil van Gogh: 'What I think of my own work is that the picture I did at Nuenen of the peasants eating potatoes is the best one after all' (W 1). 'Ma is unable to understand that painting is *a faith*,' he wrote to Theo on 5 April 1885 (398). It makes a 'mock of the holy trinity of duty, fashion and solidity' (Meyers, 52).

When a monument was unveiled to Van Gogh, a doctor-painter from Deurne remarked: 'He, Vincent van Gogh, was a man who, like most great men, was not understood and in this period did not understand himself. He still sought his gifts and sought them with a nervous earnestness. Was he not himself a missionary, teacher, healer of the sick?' (Brouwer, 129).

Millet

His great model for painting peasant life in Brabant was the French painter Jean François Millet.

Vincent somewhere mentions a self-portrait by Millet that he found attractive: 'Nothing but a head with a kind of shepherd's bonnet on it, but the look, with half-closed eyes – the intense look of a painter – how attractive that is, also that cocky look, if I may say so' (248). Vincent was very much impressed by a biography of Millet written by Alfred Sensier, *La vie et l'oeuvre de J. F. Millet,* Paris 1881, which he had got hold of (R 47) and read in The Hague. The reading of this book gave him courage (227). Sensier described Millet as a deeply religious peasant, 'who knew the Bible from the outside and in his country pictures had created a kind of biblical atmosphere' (Tilborgh, 1988, 17). When he began as a painter, he copied Millet by way of training. At the end of his life in Saint-Rémy he returned to the model of Millet. 'One began the figure of peasants and workmen as a "genre", but at present with Millet primarily as an eternal master, that is the very heart of modern art and will remain so' (418). For Vincent, Millet was synonymous with 'painting people' (Tilborgh, 1988, 5).

Via Antwerp to Paris

In November 1885 Vincent moved from Nuenen to Belgium on the way to his brother in Paris. From November 1885 to February 1886 he stayed first in Antwerp. There he worked for a while at the academy, although he took his models mostly from the port area. The discovery of the painter Rubens was one of the important things for this Antwerp period.

Already there, Vincent's study of Japanese woodcuts began; he was excited about these because of their bright colours. He was to continue this study in Paris. A canvas like 'Sheep on the Shore at Saintes-Maries' has been associated with the influence of Japanese art. In Arles he puts it like this: 'Well, isn't it almost a whole religion which is taught us by those Japanese, who are so simple and who live in nature as though they themselves were flowers? And it seems to me that people cannot study Japanese art without becoming much more alive and happier, and that this brings us back to nature despite our upbringing and our work in a conventional world' (542).

In February 1886 he went to his brother Theo in Paris and stayed there until February 1888. During this time in Paris he worked in the Cormon studio. In Paris he came under the influence of Impressionism; here special mention must be made of artists like Claude Monet, Pierre-Auguste Renoir, Henri Toulouse-Lautrec and Paul Gauguin. During his time in Paris he became particularly friendly with Gauguin and also with Emile Bernard, who was fifteen years younger. He occupied himself with pointillism.

Reference has often been made to the change which took place in Van Gogh's painting during his stay in France. His work became brighter and clearer in colour. 'Looked at superficially, this change means that the painter of the sombre range of "The Potato Eaters" suddenly came under the influence of the Paris open-air painters and thus came very close to the Impressionists and neo-Impressionists.' 'He claimed, somewhat dizzily and awkwardly, that he had been won over to the light. He painted flowers, colourful radiant Seine landscapes and yet more flowers, flowers' (Romein, 834, 835).

In the summer of 1887 he said of the feelings that he had about his vocation: 'As for me – I feel the desire for marriage and children disappearing and now and then I'm rather depressed that I should be like that as I approach thirty-five, when I ought to be feeling quite the opposite. And sometimes I blame it all on this rotten painting.' He then refers to Jean Richepin (1849–1926), a French poet and playwright, who said at one point: 'The love of art is the undoing of true love. I think that's absolutely right, but on the other hand true love makes one weary of art. And although I already feel old and broken, I can still be sufficiently in love at times to feel less passionate about painting. One must have ambition to succeed, and ambition seems to me absurd' (462).

Vincent worked in Paris like a man possessed. He painted around 200 pictures in this period. In Paris, Vincent also for the first time received some *public* recognition ('Restaurant in Paris'). From Paris he wrote in the autumn of 1886 to H. M. Livens, an English painter whom he seems to have got to know in Antwerp: 'At the present moment I've found four dealers who have exhibited studies of mine' (459a).

In *Avant et Après* Paul Gauguin related an anecdote from the Paris period. In the winter of 1886, when Vincent had gone hungry for several days, he sold some paintings for five francs. When he came out of the shop, he was accosted by 'a woman of the street'. He thought of Goncourt's 'La Fille Elisa' and gave the girl the five-franc piece (quoted from Takashina, 209).

Arles

On the advice of Toulouse-Lautrec, in February 1888 Vincent moved to Arles in Provence, where he was to remain until May 1889. He went there because of the extra 'light'. He hoped to draw new inspiration there. Indeed he was bewitched by the light and the colours, for example of blossoming fruit trees. It is from this time that the paintings of landscapes and trees in blossom come.

Perhaps it was in this period that he reached the climax of his creative existence. 'I am in a fury of work, because the trees are in blossom and I wanted to paint a Provençal orchard of astounding delight,' he wrote in the first week of April 1888 (473).

Vincent hoped there in Arles, in the 'yellow house' in which he lived and which he also painted, to found some kind of community of painters, of whom he saw Paul Gauguin as a kind of abbot (*marchand-apôtre*) (544). Gauguin's arrival so to speak announced the beginning of that.

At the end of the period in which he lived with Paul Gauguin (1848–1903) – from October to December 1888 – he suffered the first psychosis, on Christmas Eve 1888. At that time there was a dramatic break between the two friends, when on Christmas Eve Vincent threatened Paul Gauguin with a knife. In a café he poured the contents of a glass over Gauguin's head. The next evening he sat behind Gauguin in the street with an open razor. When Gauguin looked at him he turned round. He cut off a bit of his own ear and took it in an envelope to a prostitute in a brothel. Vincent was later found in bed, bleeding. He was taken into hospital, but released again on 7 January. 'Between fantasizing about philosophy and theology there were many brief moments in which he was normal' (thus Jaspers, 144). He himself says about it: 'Possible immersions in melancholy of the kind that you mention in your letter and which to which I myself fall victim now and then' (around 15 June 1888, to Wil van Gogh: W 4). 'As a matter of fact, I am again almost reduced to the madness of Hugo van der Goes in the painting by Emile Wauters (Royal Museum in Brussels) . . . Yet even then I do not think that my madness could take the form of persecution mania, since when in a state of exaltation I tend more towards thoughts of eternity and eternal life' (556).

Vincent's sickness

In the last years of his life Vincent was seriously ill. On several occasions that led to his being admitted to hospital. Between the attacks (of epilepsy) he often continued to work like a man possessed. Vincent already reckoned at an early stage that he would not have a long life. In a letter from The Hague he says that he reckoned on a period of six to ten years: '*In a few years I must complete a certain amount of work;* I needn't rush – that's no good – but I must work on in complete calmness and serenity, as regularly and with as much concentration as possible, as concisely and as pointedly as possible. The world concerns me only in so far as I have as it were a certain indebtedness and duty towards it because I have been walking around on this earth for thirty years, and out of gratitude want to leave some souvenir in the form of drawings – and paintings – not to please this or that taste in art but to express a sincere human feeling. So this work is my aim – and in concentrating on that one idea everything that one does is simplified. To this extent it isn't chaotic, but all done with one aim in mind' (309).

As early as December 1885 Vincent had incessant physical complaints. Because of a lack of money, for long periods he often ate no hot food but lived on bread and smoked, more or less to be get relief from his empty stomach. 'He lived as a kind of ascetic and allowed himself only one luxury: a pipe of tobacco,' M. J. Brusse related later (I, 113). He sometimes spoke of being 'literally exhausted'. In the years in Paris between 1886 and spring 1888 his physical state seems to have remained unsatisfactory. In Arles he quickly felt better, at least to begin with (Jaspers, 141). 'I'm beginning to feel quite a different person from what I was when I arrived here. But what a countryside!' (539).

He called his days in the hospital 'very interesting' and said that 'perhaps it is from the sick that one learns how to live' (569). Thoughts of life and death preoccupied him at this time. 'Is life as a whole visible to us, or before death do we see only one hemisphere?' (506). 'It isn't always touching for a person one knows (his uncle Vincent van Gogh had died on 28 July and his sister Wil had informed him of that) to set out on the great journey to that other hemisphere of life the existence of which we only conjecture. But it goes without saying,' Vincent writes to his sister Wil, 'that my best wishes are with the traveller' (W5). 'However, life is short, and shorter still the years when one feels strong enough to face anything' (527).

Saint-Rémy-de-Provence

From May 1889 to May 1890 Vincent lived in the mental institution of Saint-Rémy near Arles, run by Dr Peyron. In the very year that Friedrich Nietzsche, who had announced 'God is dead and we have killed him', was placed in an institution, Vincent voluntarily entered the asylum in Saint-Rémy (Edwards, 63). When he was admitted to the mental hospital he attributed his breakdowns to heredity. He was said to have had an epileptic attack, like his mother's sister. His mother's brother, Uncle Jan, committed suicide. Theo was melancholic and died in Utrecht six months after his brother during a nervous breakdown. Cor killed himself in the Transvaal during the Boer War. Wil became mentally ill around the age of forty. In 1902 she was admitted to an institution in Ermelo-Veldijk. There she died in 1941, the last of the family of Theodorus and Anna van Gogh (Meyers, 24).

Sometimes the painting of the prison exercise yard after Gustave Doré's 1885 painting, from Saint-Rémy, January/February 1889, is seen as autobiographical. The '*Ronde des prisonniers*' is said to have been an unspoken criticism of the deadening, monotonous life of patients in Saint-Paul-de-Mausole. Van Gogh is said to have copied his own features in the foremost prisoner with reddish-brown hair (Hulsker, 436, in my view wrongly, does not want to see this as a self-portrait).

On 4 January 1890 he wrote: 'At present I've been overcome with a strong feeling of despondency' (622). Around 30 April 1889 he described his condition to his sister Wil as follows: 'As for myself, I am going to an asylum in Saint-Rémy, not far from here, for three months. In all I've had four major crises, during which I had no idea what I said, wanted or did. Not counting the fact that previously I had three fainting fits for no apparent reason and without retaining the slightest recollection of what I felt at that time . . . I can't describe precisely what the matter is with me; sometimes there are horrible fits of anxiety with no apparent cause, or otherwise a feeling of emptiness and despondency in the head. I regard the whole thing more as a simple accident. No doubt much of this is my own fault, and at times I have attacks of depression and terrible remorse, but the fact is, that when all this discourages me and gives me spleen, I'm not at all embarrassed to tell myself that the remorse and guilt might perhaps have been caused by microbes, just like love. Every day I take the remedy that the incomparable Dickens prescribes against suicide. It consists of a glass of wine, a piece of bread and cheese, and a pipe of tobacco. That isn't complicated, you'll say, and you won't believe that at some moments melancholy so overcomes me that I can't get rid of it – oh dear . . . Well, it isn't always pleasant, but I do my best not to forget altogether how to make jokes about it. I try to avoid anything to do with hero-ism or martyrdom; in short, I try not to look on lugubrious things from the lugubrious side' (W 11). And in the next letter to her: 'Although it's with obstinate ingratitude that I feel my health gradually returning, the fact is that I'm quite well. However, as I say, the inclination to take up the joys of life again is not very great' (W 12). From Saint-Rémy, around 9 June 1889 he wrote to his brother Theo that his brain was 'showing some sort of derangement; it's bewildering in this way to be fearful about nothing, and not to be able to remem-ber things' (594).

'It is in learning to suffer without complaining, in learning to look on pain without repugnance, that one risks vertigo. Yet it is possible that one may even catch a glimpse of a vague probability that on the other side of life we shall see good reason for the existence of pain, which seen from here some-times so fills our whole horizon that it takes on the pro-portions of a hopeless flood. We know very little about this, about its proportions, and it is better to look at a wheatfield, even in the form of a painting' (Saint-Rémy, 2 July 1889, 597).

Auvers-sur-Oise

From May 1890, Vincent spent the last two months of his life in Auvers, near Paris. It was Theo who had put Vincent in contact with the artistic Dr Gachet. On Theo's advice, Vincent lived in 'freedom' under the supervision of this doctor. Vincent called Dr Gachet himself 'very nervous and even very bizarre' (W 22). This doctor, who had lost his wife shortly before Vincent had made his acquaintance, had 'gained his doctorate with a thesis on melancholia in which he paid a good deal of attention to the melancholic temperament of the artist' (Van Uitert, 1983, 57, 94). That means that he wrote the book before he treated Vincent van Gogh! After a short time with his brother and his wife in Paris, Vincent went to Auvers (May–July 1890). Vincent also painted Dr Gachet and his daughter. Van Gogh himself said of the portrait of Dr Gachet: 'It . . . has an expression of melancholy' (W 23). To paint a melancholy portrait of Dr Gachet is to paint Christ for our time (Edwards, 28).

We can see from Vincent van Gogh's last letters how he wrestled with the question of the meaning of his existence (as a painter). He referred back to an expression from his first period. In the last letter which Vincent sent from Dordrecht, he mentioned that during a morning service in the French church he heard a sermon on I Cor. 13.12: 'For we now see through a glass darkly' (94). Vincent appropriately enough returns to this text at the end of his life in a letter to his mother. Rather more than a month before his death he wrote: 'As though through a looking glass, by a dark reason – so it has remained; life and the why of saying farewell and going away and the continuance of unrest, one does not understand more of it than that. For me life might well continue being iso-lated. Those to whom I've been most attached, I've seen only through a looking glass, by a dark reason. And yet there is a reason for there occasionally being more harmony in my work now. Painting is something in itself. Last year I read somewhere that writing a book or painting a picture was like having a child. However, I daren't claim that – I've always thought that the latter was the more natural and the best. So I say, only *if* it were so, only *if* it were the same' (641a). And in another letter: 'At present I am feeling much calmer than last year, and really the restlessness in my head has greatly calmed down. In fact, I've always really believed that seeing the surroundings of the old days would have this effect' (650).

In Auvers he wrote to his brother and his wife Jo about the illness of their child: 'I have just received the letter in which you say that the child is ill; I should greatly like to come and see you, and what holds me back is the thought that I should be even more powerless than you in the present state of sorrow . . .' (1 July 1890, 646).

Public recognition

Some months before Vincent's death, for the first time an appreciation of his work appeared in the press. In January 1890 the critic Albert Aurier (1865–1892) wrote a review in the *Mercure de France* in which he described the paintings of Van Gogh as the exalted work of a great painter and dreamer: 'Will this strong and truthful artist, who is so much of the true race, with the powerful hands of a giant, with the nervous system of a hysterical woman, with the soul of a seer, so original and standing by himself in the midst of the wretched art of the present time – will this artist one day – everything is possible – know the joy of a first exhibition, the contrite coaxing of fashion? Perhaps. But whatever may happen, even if it should become fashionable to pay for his canvases – though this is not very probable – the prices asked for the petty nothings by M. Meissonier, even then I do not feel that much honesty can ever have a place in this late admiration of the great public. Vincent van Gogh is both too simple and too subtle for the present-day bourgeois spirit. He will never be fully understood except by his brothers, the artists who are really artists to the full, and by fortunate ones among the little people, the very little people' (Albert Aurier, 'Les isolés. Vincent van Gogh', *Mercure de France*, January 1890; cf. Hulsker, 1988, 543).

But Vincent responded to this outburst of praise with touching modesty. 'I was extremely surprised by the article on my pictures which you sent me. I needn't tell you that I hope to go on thinking that I do not paint like that, but I do see in it how I must paint' (625). 'Please ask M. Aurier not to write any more articles on my painting. Tell him emphatically that in the first place he is mistaken about me and that moreover I really am too deeply sunk in grief to be able to face publicity. Making pictures distracts me, but if I hear them spoken of, it pains me more than he knows,' he wrote to Theo (629).

To his sister he wrote: 'But when I had read that article I felt almost mournful, for I thought: I ought to be like that, and I feel so inferior' (W 20). And to his mother and sister he said: 'As soon as I heard that my work was having some success, and read the article in question, I feared at once that I should be punished for it; for this is how things nearly always go in a painter's life: success is about the worst thing that can happen' (629a).

To Albert Aurier Vincent himself wrote: 'However, I feel uneasy in my mind when I reflect that what you say is due to others rather than to myself. For example, Monticelli in particular' (Vincent to Albert Aurier, 626a).

Vincent's death

Vincent's illness did not stop him working. Around 20 March 1890 in Saint-Rémy he wrote: 'The work went well, the last canvas of branches in blossom – you will see that it was perhaps the best, the most patiently worked thing I had done, painted with calm and with a great firmness of touch' (628).

'The more ugly, old, vicious, sick, poor I get, the more I want to take my revenge by producing brilliant colours, well arranged, resplendent' (W 7). On his own account, in the last period of his stay there he worked like a man in a frenzy, especially on bunches of flowers and violet irises (4/5 June 1890, W 22).

On 25 July Theo wrote to his wife after receiving a letter from Vincent in which he detected the approaching crisis: 'When will a happy time dawn for him? And he is so good through and through' (Miedema, 79).

The thought of suicide must have long been familiar to Vincent. In one of his very first letters to Theo Vincent wrote: 'Theo, I must recommend that you begin to smoke a pipe; it's so good if you ever get depressed, as still keeps happening to me at present' (5). Perhaps it is not a complete coincidence that several times he painted pipes in his pictures. One might think of Vincent's 'Chair with Pipe and Books', December 1888–January 1889, or 'Still Life on the Table with Book, Pipe, Candlestand, Letter and Eggs', January 1889. (This last painting contains the *Annuaire de la Santé,* a book which belonged to Dr Rey, who treated him in Saint-Rémy.)

In Amsterdam, when he was attempting to pass the state examination he referred again to Dickens' advice to those who had such tendencies: 'Have a bite to eat, a piece of bread and a glass of beer, that is a remedy that Dickens recommends to those who are on the point of committing suicide, as being very effective for dissuading them from their purpose, at least for a while' (106). On 6 July 1882, when he had spent the summer in hospital in The Hague for the treatment of a venereal disease, he wrote: 'There was some inexpressible melancholy in me at that time which is impossible for me to describe. I know that then I thought a good deal of a manly word of Father Millet: "It has always seemed to me that suicide was the action of a dishonourable man." The emptiness, the inexpressible wretchedness made me think: I can understand that there are people who jump into the water.

Only it was far from me to approve such a thing in those men, I found solidity in that saying that I wrote to you, that it was far better to grasp at a better view of life and seek a remedy in work' (212). A year before his death Vincent had written to his brother Theo: 'If I didn't have your friendship, I would be inexorably driven to suicide, and however cowardly I am, I should end by doing it' (588).

In an accompanying letter of 3/4 September 1889 Dr Peyron could clearly still (or again) write to Theo: 'His thoughts of suicide have disappeared, only disturbing dreams remain, but they tend to disappear too, and their intensity is already less great' (602a).

On 27 July 1890 the crisis came. Vincent shot himself in the chest, leaning against a tree. He did not die immediately, but was still able to get home. 'When he got home he was asked, "But M. Vincent, where have you come from, what's happened?" "I'd had enough and then I killed myself!" I saw him on his narrow bed in the attic, a prey to terrible pains. Is there no one to open my belly? It was scorching hot under that roof. Already smoking, he was having conversations with Dr Gachet. He said nothing about his motives for his suicide. When Dr Gachet asked him, he shrugged his shoulders' (Jaspers, 147). Two days later, on a Monday evening, 19 July 1890, he died smoking his pipe, in the presence of his brother Theo. According to a letter from Theo to his sister Elizabeth his last words were: 'La tristesse durera toujours' (Hulsker, 585).

In Auvers, in the room where Vincent was laid out, his last paintings were hung along the walls, including the Pietà after Delacroix and the 'Prisoners at Exercise' after Gustave Doré. They shone like a halo. Over the bier lay a white sheet with many flowers, *sunflowers* and other *yellow* flowers (IV, 338).

There has been some speculation as to what the painter Raphael could have painted had he lived as long as Michelangelo. Vincent van Gogh lived no longer than Raphael. Certainly he has left behind an enormous *oeuvre*.

Despite the fact that he had only ten years as a painter, he bequeathed a gigantic legacy: more than 8000 paintings and 1500 drawings. He wrote around 850 letters. He had the last on him when he died. Theo's widow, Jo Bonger, edited this correspondence in 1914.

Theo: comrade

In his last letter, which he carried with him unposted, Vincent van Gogh wrote, among other things: 'But yet, my dear brother, there is this that I have always told you, and I repeat it once more with all the earnestness that can be expressed by the effort of a mind firmly fixed on trying to do as well as possible – I tell you again that I shall always consider you to be something more than a simple dealer in Corots, that through my mediation you have your share in the actual production of some canvases, which will retain their calm even in the catastrophe . . . Well, my own work, I'm risking my life for it and my reason has half-foundered because of it. That's all right, but you are not among the dealers in men . . .' (652).

After Vincent's death Theo wrote to his mother: 'One cannot write how sorrowful one is, or find comfort. It is a pain which will weigh with me long and which will certainly never leave my thoughts for the rest of my life, but if one should want to say anything it is that he himself has the rest that he longed for. Life weighed so heavy on him, but as things are, *now* everyone is full of praise for his talent. O mother, he was so much my brother' (I, xlix). Six months later – on 25 January 1891 – Vincent's 'comrade' died in Utrecht. Many years later his wife Jo van Gogh-Bonger had his material remains brought to France. In her introduction to the edition of the letters, she wrote: 'They rest together in the little cemetery among the grainfields at Auvers' (I, xxix). This is close to the church that Vincent painted. Ivy now unites the two graves. On 29 July 1990, a century after his death, the fields around the little cemetery were full of sunflowers in bloom.

2

Vincent as Preacher and Evangelist

'Once when I was in Paris, Pa sent me (by De Genestet)
... *'There is No Priest Who Explains Him'* (87)

Aspiration to become a preacher

Vincent's father was a preacher in predominantly Roman-Catholic Brabant, in places like Zundert, Etten and Nuenen, where he eventually died. Vincent had a great love and affection for his father. He very much wanted to work within the framework of the church.

Although Theo had suggested to Vincent earlier than 1880 the possibility of becoming a painter, initially Vincent would not listen. His father suggested to him the possibility of going to work in a museum or beginning in the art business. Although initially Vincent did work in the art trade in The Hague, London and Paris, in 1876 he went to England in response to an advertisement. He wrote from Etten on 4 April 1876: 'On the morning before I left Paris, I received a letter from a schoolmaster in Ramsgate. He proposed that I go there for a month (without salary); at the end of that time he will see whether he can use me. You can imagine I'm glad to have found something. At all events I have board and lodging free' (59).

In April 1876 he accepted a post with Mr Thomas Slade Stokes in Ramsgate. This Congregationalist preacher ran a boarding school which in July was moved to Holmes Court, Isleworth. He also took church services. Mr Slade's school was not a large one. It had a sea view, as is witnessed by the drawings which Vincent made of it: 'Some – of the boys – will never forget the view from the window (which made them forget the many bugs)' (72) . . . 'On such days Mr Stokes is sometimes in a bad temper, and if he feels that the boys are being too lively, they have to go without their supper. I wish you could see them looking from the window then, it is rather melancholy. They have so little else except their meals to look forward to and to help them pass their days' (67). Vincent worked for Mr Stokes from July to December 1876.

From Welwyn, a village north of London, about twenty-five miles from Isleworth, where he was visiting his sister, he wrote: 'I stayed two days in London and have been running from one part to another to see different persons, including a minister to whom I had written . . . If I should find anything, it will probably be a position between preacher and missionary among the working people in the suburbs of London' (Welwyn, 17 June 1876, 69).

We can discover something of his situation from the content of the letter to the English preacher that he sent with the letter just mentioned:

Reverend Sir,
A preacher's son who, as he has to work for his living, has neither the time nor the money to study at King's College, and who besides is already a few years beyond the age at which one usually enters there and has as yet not even begun preparatory studies in Latin and Greek, would nevertheless be happy to find a position related to the church, though the position of a preacher with a college training is beyond his reach . . . But as my aim is a situation in connection with the church, I must look for something else. Though I have not been educated for the church, perhaps my travels, my life in different countries, mixing with various people, poor and rich, religious and irreligious, and different kinds of work – manual labour and office work – perhaps also my speaking a number of languages, may partly make up for the fact that I have not studied. But the

reason which I would rather give for introducing myself to you is my innate love for the church and everything connected with it. It may have slumbered now and then, but is always roused again. Also, if I may say so, though with a feeling of great insufficiency and shortcoming, 'The love of God and man.' And when I think of my past life and my father's home in the Dutch village, there comes to me the feeling of, 'Father, I have sinned against heaven, and before you, and am no more worthy to be called your son: make me as one of your hired servants. Be merciful to me, a sinner.' When I lived in London, I often went to church to hear you, and have not forgotten you. Now I ask your recommendation in looking for a position, and also for you to keep your fatherly eye on me if I find such a position. I have been left very much to myself, and I think your fatherly eye will do me good (Ramsgate, June 1876, 69a).

During a visit to London he related how he had heard talk of preachers in Liverpool who often needed auxiliary preachers who could speak various languages in order to work among the seamen and among foreigners, and also to visit the sick. Such a job also carried a salary (75).

Also because of the sober conditions on which he was accepted – no salary – he looked for other work and got it, also in Isleworth, from a Methodist preacher, Mr Thomas Slade Jones, although he asked himself where Mr Jones himself got his income from. Mr Jones gave him the opportunity to be a kind of auxiliary preacher (cf. I, xxii, xxiii). In a letter he writes: 'Mr Jones has promised me that I shall not have to teach so much in future, but may work more in his community, visiting the people, talking with them etc. May God give it his blessing' (76).

As later in the Borinage, Vincent was aware of the circumstances in which the people among whom he lived worked: 'There is such a longing for religion among the people in the big cities. Many a labourer in a factory or shop has had a distinctive, beautiful, pious childhood. But city life takes away the "early dew of morning". Still, the longing for the "old, old story" remains; whatever is at the bottom of the heart stays there. In one of her books, George Eliot describes the life of factory workers who have formed a small community and hold their services in a chapel in Lantern Yard. She calls it "the kingdom of God on earth" – no more and no less' (66).

The content of his ministry

Vincent gave the following description of the content of his work: 'Lately it has seemed to me that there are no professions in the world other than those of schoolmaster and preacher, with all that lies between these two – such as missionary, London missionary, etc. I think it must be a peculiar profession to be a London missionary; one has to go around among the workers and the poor to spread the Bible, and as soon as one has some experience, talk with them, find foreigners who are looking for work or other persons who are in difficulties and try and help them, etc., etc. Last week I went to London several times to find out if there was a chance of becoming one of them. As I speak a number of languages and have mixed, especially in Paris and London, with people of the lower class and foreigners, and am a foreigner myself, I thought I might be suitable for it and might become increasingly so. However, one must be at least twenty-four years old, and so at all events I shall have to wait another year. Mr Stokes says that he definitely can't give me any salary because he can get teachers for just board and lodging, and that is true. But will it be possible for me to continue this way? I'm afraid not; it will be decided soon enough. But, my dear chap, however things turn out, I can tell you that these few months have bound me so strongly to the sphere that extends from schoolmaster to preacher, both by the pleasures connected with those professions and by the thorns which have pricked me, that I cannot draw back. So I have to go on! I can assure you that some very peculiar difficulties will present themselves right away, and others are looming in the distance. One is in quite a different world from that of Messrs Goupil & Co' (Isleworth, 5 July 1876, 70).

In his work he often discussed Bible stories with the young people. 'Every morning and evening we read the Bible and sing and pray. And that is a good thing. At Ramsgate we did the same, and when those twenty-one boys from the London markets and streets pray, "Our Father who art in heaven, give us this day our daily bread," I have often thought of the cry of the young ravens to which the Lord listens, and it did me good to pray with them and to bend my head lower than they probably did at the words, "Lead us not into temptation, but deliver us from evil"' (73; cf. also 74).

Vincent's sermons

It is possible to give a picture of the content of Vincent's preaching, both the themes that he treated and the texts that he chose.

In a letter to his mother we read: 'Last Monday I was again in Richmond, and took as my text, "He has sent me to preach the gospel to the poor." But anyone who wants to preach the gospel must carry it in his own heart first. O that I may find it, for it is only the word spoken in simplicity and from the abundance of the heart that can bear fruit' (77). On 10 November 1876 he wrote from Isleworth: 'Monday evening I hope to go to Richmond again, and to choose for my text the words, "But when he was still a long way off, his father saw him, and had compassion." Theo, woe is me if I do not preach the gospel – if I did not aim at that and possess faith and hope in Christ, it would be bad for me indeed; but now I have some *courage*' (80). Vincent related how on a particular occasion in Turnham Green he preached on the text: "I would to God that not only you, but also all those who hear me this day, were as I, except for these bonds." Next Sunday evening I have to go to a Methodist church in Petersham. Petersham is a village by the Thames, twenty minutes beyond Richmond. I don't know what text I shall take, The Prodigal Son or Psalm 42.1. In the morning and afternoon there is Sunday School at Turnham Green . . . Tomorrow I must be in the two remotest parts of London: in Whitechapel, that very poor part you have read about in Dickens; and then across the Thames in a little steamer and from there to Lewisham' (81). In yet another letter he wrote about his choice of the text Acts 5.14–16: 'And more than ever believers were added to the Lord, multitudes both of men and women, so that they even carried out the sick into the streets, and laid them on beds and pallets, that as Peter came by at least his shadow might fall on some of them. The people also gathered from the towns around Jerusalem, bringing the sick and those afflicted with unclean spirits, and they were all healed' – and Acts 12.5–17: Peter in prison and his miraculous liberation (82).

In a letter from the first half of November 1876 Vincent wrote to Theo about the first sermon that he had given in the Methodist church in Richmond, presumably on 5 November: 'Theo, your brother has preached for the first time, last Sunday, in God's house, of which it is written: "In this place I will give peace." Enclosed is a copy of what I said. May it be the first of many' (79).

Vincent sent the text of his sermon – of course in English – with the letter to Theo. The text which he had chosen as the theme of his sermon was Psalm 119.19: 'I am a stranger on earth, do not hide your commandments from me,' very much in keeping with his own consciousness of working as a foreigner among foreigners.

'. . . It is a glorious thought that from now on wherever I go I shall preach the gospel; to do that *well*, one must have the gospel in one's heart. May the Lord give it to me. You know enough of the world, Theo, to understand that a *poor* preacher stands quite alone in the world, but the Lord can increasingly rouse in us the consciousness and trust of faith: "Yet I am not alone, for the Father is with me."

> I know to whom I trust myself,
> Though day and night may alternate.
> I know the rock on which I build;
> He does not fail who awaits your salvation.'

Vincent quoted the last verse of the hymn 'I will give thanks to you, O God', along with other verses from the psalms and hymns. A text from Genesis is also inscribed between the lines: 'God said, "Let there be light." And there was light' (79) (cf. Hulsker, 1988, 21).

After quoting the text from Ps.119.19 he begins the sermon as follows:

> *It is an old belief and it is a good belief, that our life is a pilgrim's progress – that we are strangers on the earth, but that though this be so, yet we are not alone, for our Father is with us. We are pilgrims, our life is a long walk or journey from earth to Heaven. The beginning of this life is this: there is only one who remembers no more her sorrow and her anguish for joy that a man is born into the world. She is our mother. The end of our pilgrimage is the entering in Our Father's house, where are many mansions, where he has gone before us to prepare a place for us. The end of this life is what we call death – it is an hour in which words are spoken, things are seen and felt, that are kept in the secret chambers of the hearts of those who stand by . . . There is sorrow in the hour when a man is born into the world, but also joy, deep and unspeakable, thankfulness so great that it reaches the highest Heavens. Yes the angels of God, they smile, they hope and they rejoice when a man is born in the world. There is sorrow in the hour of death, but there is also joy unspeakable when it is the hour of death of one who*

has fought a good fight. There is one who has said: I am the resurrection and the life, if any man believe in me, though he were dead, yet shall he live. There was an apostle who heard a voice from heaven saying, Blessed are they that die in the Lord, for they rest from their labour and their works follow them.

. . . Sorrow is better than joy – and even in mirth the heart is sad – and it is better to go to the house of mourning than to the house of feasts . . .

We are pilgrims on the earth and strangers – we come from afar and we are going far. The journey of our life goes from the loving breast of our Mother on earth to the arms of our Father in heaven. Everything on earth changes – we have no abiding city here – it is the experience of everybody.

When Vincent had spoken about journeys on the sea and through storms, with references, among others, to Psalm 107 and the story of the storm from John 6.17–21, he went on to say:

My peace I leave with you – we saw how there is peace even in the storm. Thanks be to God, who has given us to be born and to live in a Christian country. Has any one of us forgotten the golden hours of our early days at home, and since we left that home – for many of us have had to leave that home and to earn their living and to make their way in the world. Has he not brought us thus far? Have we lacked anything? Lord, we believe, help Thou our unbelief. I still feel the rapture, the thrill of joy I felt when for the first time I cast a deep look in the lives of my parents, when I felt by instinct how much they were Christians. And I still feel that feeling of eternal youth and enthusiasm wherewith I went to God, saying, 'I will be a Christian too.'

In the letter to Theo mentioned above, Vincent referred to a painting to which he alluded in his sermon from England: 'Did

I ever tell you about that picture by (George Henry) Boughton, "The Pilgrim's Progress"? It is towards evening. A sandy path leads over the hills to a mountain, on the top of which is the Holy City, lit by the red sun setting behind the grey evening clouds. On the road is a pilgrim who wants to go to the city; he is already tired and asks a woman in black, who is standing by the road and whose name is "Sorrowful yet always rejoicing":

Does the road go uphill then all the way? .
Yes to the very end.
And will the journey take all day long?'
From morn till night, my friend' (74).

These last lines come from a poem 'Uphill' by the poet Christina Rossetti (1830–1894), whom he very much admired (41; 112). In the sermon he puts it like this:

Our life is a pilgrim's progress. I once saw a very beautiful picture: it was a landscape at evening. In the distance on the right-hand side a row of hills appeared blue in the evening mist. Above those hills the splendour of the sunset, the grey clouds with their linings of silver and gold and purple. The landscape is a plain or heath covered with grass and its yellow leaves, for it was in autumn. Through the landscape a road leads to a high mountain far, far away; on the top of that mountain is a city whereon the setting sun casts a glory. On the road walks a pilgrim, staff in hand. He has been walking for a good long while already and he is very tired. And now he meets a woman, or figure in black, that makes one think of St Paul's word: As being sorrowful yet always rejoicing. That angel of God has been placed there to encourage the pilgrims and to answer their questions and the pilgrim asks her: 'Does the road go uphill then all the way?' And the answer is: 'Yes to the very end.'

And he asks again: 'And will the journey take all day

long?' And the answer is: 'From morn till night, my friend.'
    *And the pilgrim goes on sorrowful yet always rejoicing –
sorrowful because it is so far off and the road so long.
Hopeful as he looks up to the eternal city far away, resplendent in the evening glow.*

Vincent ends his sermon:

*And when each of us goes back to the daily things and daily
duties, let us not forget that things are not what they
seem, that God by the things of daily life teaches us higher
things, that our life is a pilgrim's progress, and that we are
strangers on the earth, but that we have a God and Father
who preserves strangers, and that we are all brothers* (I,
88–91).

From the imagery that he uses in this sermon it becomes
clear how much, apart from reading the Bible itself, Vincent is
influenced by reading John Bunyan's *Pilgrim's Progress* and of
course also Thomas à Kempis's *The Imitation of Christ*.

Dordrecht

When Vincent was working as a messenger boy in a bookshop
in Dordrecht, however, the thought of being a preacher would
not let him go. 'I believe and trust that my life will be changed
somehow, and that this longing for him will be satisfied. I too
am sometimes sad and lonely, especially when I'm near a
church or manse. Let's not give in, but try to be gentle and
patient' (Dordrecht, 16 March 1877: 88). He steeped himself
intensively in the Bible, for which he sometimes says he longs
very much (88). 'In the first place I think of the saying, "It is
my portion to keep your words"; I have such a longing to
possess the treasure of the Bible, to study thoroughly and
lovingly all those old stories, and especially to find out what
is known of Christ' (89). Vincent then points out that in his

family, 'which is a Christian family in every sense, there
has always been, from generation to generation, one who
preached the gospel. Why shouldn't a member of that family
feel himself called to that service now, and why shouldn't he
have reason to believe that he may and must declare his intentions and seek the means to reach that goal? It is my prayer
and fervent desire that the spirit of my father and grandfather
may rest upon me, that it may be given me to become a
Christian and a Christian labourer, and that my life may
resemble more and more the lives of those named above; for
behold, the old wine is good, and I do not desire new wine . . .
If only I were through with this long and difficult study to
become a preacher of the gospel. Look, Pa can count his
religious practices and Bible readings and visits to the sick
and poor and his written sermons by the thousands, and still
he doesn't just look around, but goes to do good. Raise your
eyes above for me too and wish that it may be granted me . . .'
(89).

In a letter of 23 April 1877 from Dordrecht Vincent already
alluded to going to Amsterdam to study theology. Uncle Jan,
who lived in Amsterdam, had been in Etten and had said that
his room was already prepared: 'In May I shall probably be
able to put my hand to the plough. I will hang the prints you
gave me in that little room, and so they will remind me of you
daily . . . I suppose that for a "sower of God's word", as I hope
to be, as well as for a sower of the seed in the fields, every day
will bring enough of its own evil, and the earth will produce
many thorns and thistles. Let us continue to help each other
and ask for brotherly love' (93).

Vincent was not directly encouraged to take this course by
those around him in Dordrecht. The son of the bookseller
with whom he worked in the shop, Mr D. Braat, later related:
'For at that time he had again got it into his head that he
wanted to work as a minister. The Revd Keller van Hoorn was
in his prime in Dordt, and Van Gogh went to ask his advice.
But he found the preliminary studies too hard . . . Not that he

didn't work hard enough at them, but he had never been to a grammar school. Mr van Hoorn then wanted to encourage him to be a missionary, but Vincent wasn't interested in that. He preferred to go to study. His father was also a preacher. "I want to be a pastor, just like Pa," he said to me one day. "My dear chap," I warned him, "don't you think it sad that after so many years your father has got no further than Etten and Leur?" That's really the only time I have seen Van Gogh cross. It was just the right place for his father, the true pastor. Well, a short time later Vincent went to Amsterdam and was taken into the home of his uncle the rear admiral, where he began to study Latin and Greek in a rented room' (I, 109).

Study in Amsterdam

From May 1877 Vincent stayed in Amsterdam to prepare for the state examination there. A knowledge of Latin and Greek were a necessary condition of studying theology. That alone could open the way for him to the study of theology and training as a preacher. His Uncle Jan van Gogh, at that moment the director of the dockyard, with whom he had lodgings, was a widower; his children were already grown up and out of the house. His uncle the Revd Mr Stricker kept an eye on his studies. This uncle introduced him to Dr Mendes da Costa, a teacher of classical languages. Da Costa lived in the Jewish quarter of Amsterdam (101). Another member of the family, Uncle Cor, had an art business in Leidsestraat in Amsterdam.

From Vincent's letter it is clear how he continued to maintain his ideal of becoming a preacher despite all the difficulties: 'You know what I want. If I may become a preacher and fill the position so that my work resembles that of our father, then I shall thank God. I have a good hope: once someone more advanced in life than I am and who was no stranger to Jerusalem said to me, "I believe that you are a Christian!" It did me so much good to hear that word' (99). 'May God give me the wisdom I need and grant me what I so fervently desire

– that is, to finish my studies as quickly as possible and be ordained, so that I can do the practical work of a preacher' (113). 'As for me, I must become a good preacher who has something to say that is good and can be useful in the world; perhaps it's good that I have a relatively long time of preparation and am strongly confirmed in a deep conviction before I am called to speak to others about it . . . Even in the most civilized circles and the best surroundings and circumstances, one must keep something of the original character of a Robinson Crusoe or natural man, for otherwise one has no root in oneself, and one must never let the fire in one's soul go out, but keep it burning. And whoever chooses poverty for himself and loves it, possesses a great treasure and will always hear the voice of his conscience clearly; he who hears and obeys that voice in his innermost depths, which is the best gift of God, finds at last a friend in it, and is never alone . . . One cannot do better than hold on to the thought of God through everything, in all circumstances, at all places, at all times, and try to come to know him more, both from the Bible and from all other things. It is good to continue believing that everything is more miraculous than one can comprehend, for that is the truth; it is good to remain sensitive and humble and tender of heart, even though sometimes one has to hide this feeling, for that is often necessary; it is good to be learned in the things that are hidden from the wise and understanding in the world but are revealed, as if by nature, to the poor and simple, to women and little children. For what can one learn that is better than what God has given by nature to every human soul – which lives and loves, hopes and believes, in the depth of every soul, unless it is wantonly destroyed?' (121).

But the actual study for the state examination gave Vincent many headaches. 'The study is very difficult, dear chap, but I must keep on' (102). 'At present I'm collecting Latin and Greek topics and all kinds of writings about history, etc. I'm doing one about the Reformation now, and it's getting quite lengthy' (103). Of course for the admission examination he

had to do not only Latin and Greek but also algebra, math-
ematics, history, geography and Dutch (113). Thus Vincent
related that he had made an extract of the history of the
Reformation (102), from which it appears that he was not
only occupied with the study of the classics. 'Last week for a
change I made a précis of Paul's journeys and drew a map.
That's worth having' (105). 'I wrote a paper in which all the
parables are arranged in order and the miracles, etc.' (106).

He hoped with God's help to pass the examination. His
teacher in classics, Mendes da Costa, had given him every
hope that at the end of three months he would get as far as
Mendes had proposed, if things went well. 'But Greek lessons
in the heart of Amsterdam, in the heart of the Jewish quarter,
on a very close and sultry summer afternoon, with the feeling
that many difficult examinations hang over my head, arranged
by learned and shrewd professors, I can tell you they make one
feel more oppressed than the Brabant cornfields, which by
now must be beautiful on such a day. But as Uncle Jan says,
we must keep "pushing on"' (103). Although Vincent found
learning Latin and Greek difficult, he said that he still felt
happy. His uncle had forbidden him to work too late into
the evening. 'I shall be too glad for words if I can pass my
examination; if I can overcome the difficulties, it will be in all
simplicity of heart but also in prayer to God, for I often pray
fervently to him for the wisdom I need . . . And then that he
may one day grant that I write and preach many sermons – the
more the better – like our father's, and finish a work in my life,
with every day bringing some improvement' (112). 'Old
fellow, if next Christmas I were at the academy and had overcome the first difficulties, as I am now over the beginnings of
Latin and Greek, how happy I should be' (115).

Relations with Mendes da Costa

In his letters Vincent has written about his relationship to Mendes da Costa, while we also know what opinion Mendes da Costa had of his pupil Vincent van Gogh.

Vincent thought that his teacher Mendes da Costa bore a certain likeness to the lithograph of Thomas à Kempis, 'L'Imitation de Jésus Christ', by the Spanish portrait painter Luis Ruyperez (1833–1867; cf. 33, 106). He was very preoccupied with Thomas à Kempis's book at that time and it also played a role in the relationship between them. Vincent relates that he had sent a copy of Thomas à Kempis's *The Imitation of Christ* to Mendes da Costa and had written in it: 'In him there is neither Jew nor Greek, slave nor free, male nor female, but Christ is all and in all' (116).

Once he had had a conversation with Mendes over the words of Jesus, about '"whoever does not hate his own life cannot be my disciple". Mendes asserted that that expression was too strong, but I held that it was the simple truth; and doesn't Thomas à Kempis say the same thing when he speaks about knowing oneself and hating oneself? When we look at others who have done more than we have and are better than we are, we very soon begin to hate our own life because it is not as good as others'. Look at a man like Thomas à Kempis, who wrote his little book with a simplicity and sincerity unequalled by any other writer, before or since . . .' (116).

Twenty years after Vincent's death, in 1910, Dr M. B. Mendes da Costa recalled the following about his pupil Vincent: 'First acquaintance, which is so important for the teacher-pupil relationship, was very pleasant. There was relatively little age-difference between me and this young man who was apparently so gauche: I was then twenty-six and he was certainly already more than twenty. He immediately felt at his ease and I liked the look of him, despite his long sandy hair and many freckles. In passing it should be said that I don't quite understand how his sister can talk of "his more or less rough appearance"; it is possible that, since I never saw him again, because of his slovenliness, perhaps because he let his beard grow, his appearance lost something of its former charming strangeness, but it was certainly never rough. That wasn't true either of his nervous hands or of that face which, while certainly ugly, was still so eloquent and which hid still more.

I very soon came to win his trust and his friendship, which was so very necessary here, and as he was intent on beginning his studies, with the best intentions, in the beginning we made good progress, so that before long I could get him translating an easy Latin author. Needless to say, with his enthusiastic nature at that time, he immediately began to apply that bit of knowledge of Latin to reading Thomas à Kempis in the original . . .

But he didn't want to succeed with Greek. "Mendes," he said – we called each other by name – "Mendes, do you really believe that such horrors are necessary for someone who wants what I want: to give peace to poor creatures in their existence on earth?" And I, who of course as his teacher could not admit that he was right, but in the depth of my soul thought that he – note, I say he, Vincent van Gogh – was quite right, defended myself as skilfully as possible. But it didn't work.

"John Bunyan's *The Pilgrim's Progress* is far more useful for me and Thomas à Kempis and a translation of the Bible; I don't need more." I don't know how many times he said that to me, and how many times I went to see the Revd Mr Stricker to discuss the matter; after which, time and again it was decided that Vincent would try just once more.' Mendes da Costa related how Vincent chastized himself if he did not succeed in his work: 'Mendes, I used the stick again last night.'

'I can still see him – at that time I was living on the Jonas Daniël Meyerplein and my study was three floors up – crossing from the bridge over the Nieuwe Heerengracht, without an overcoat, as a kind of self-chastisement, with the books under his right arm pressed against his body, and holding in his left hand in front of his chest the snowdrops (which he had picked for Mendes on the Oosterbegraafplaats, his favour place for walking), his head bent a little to the right, while with the corners of his mouth pulled down, an indescribable expression of sadness and despair came over his face. And when he got upstairs, again that distinctive, deep melancholy low voice remarked: 'Mendes, don't be cross with me; I've brought a few flowers for you because you're so good to me.'

It seems to me it would have been impossible for anyone to be cross with him, and not just for me, who had come to understand how in those days he was as it were consumed by his need to help the unfortunate. I had noticed that even in my house: not only was he very interested in my deaf-mute brother, but he also always had a friendly word for and about a slightly deformed aunt, with no means, who lived with us, who was slow to understand and had difficulty in speaking, so that many people mocked her. This aunt tried to make herself of use by what people call "answering the bell", and when she saw Vincent arriving, she hastened to the street door as fast as her old legs would carry her and welcome him with a "Good morning, Mr van Gort". "Mendes," Vincent would then often say, "although that aunt of yours pronounces my name in such a strange way, she has a good soul: I'm very fond of her."'

Mendes da Costa related that they often spoke about Vincent's former business: 'the art trade'. 'He still had a number of prints from those days, lithographs after paintings and so on. He repeatedly brought me one of them, but always totally spoilt because he literally scribbled round the white borders with quotations from Thomas à Kempis and from the Bible which had more or less some relation to the subject. Once he even gave me a copy of *The Imitation of Christ* as a gift, but by no means with the unspoken intention of trying to convert me; he wanted to acquaint me with only the humanity in it.

In no way could I guess in those days, any more than anyone other than himself, that in the depths of his soul lay the embryo of the future visionary of colour.

I just remember this: proud that I could do it with the money that I earned myself, I had replaced a Turkish carpet which was at least fifty years old and worn to the threads with a modest but new rug: "Mendes," said Vincent, when he saw it, "I would never have thought that of you! Do you really think that it's more attractive than those old faded colours, of which there were so many?" And Mendes was ashamed; he felt that this marvellous young man was right.

Our relationship lasted just a year. Then I became convinced that he would never be able to pass the examination he wanted to . . . At least a year before that would have been possible, even with the utmost effort on his part, at Vincent's request, on the advice of his uncle, I let him stop. And that was that' (112a; I, 169–171).

A year later Vincent had a very negative view of the time of his studies in Amsterdam. 'My memory of that time in Amsterdam is still so fresh. You were there yourself, so you know how things were planned and discussed, argued and considered, talked over with wisdom, with the best intentions, and yet how miserable the result was, how ludicrous the whole undertaking, how utterly foolish. I still shudder when I think of it. It was the worst time that I've experienced' (Petit-Wasmes, midway through August 1879, 132).

Training as an evangelist in Belgium

When the way towards becoming a preacher was closed to him in Amsterdam, on the advice of his father, Vincent went to Belgium. His aspiration to bring people the comfort of the gospel remained. There in Brussels he could train as an evangelist, since there was no requirement for knowledge of ancient languages. Before he went there he again spent a short time with his parents in Etten. From there he wrote on 22 July 1878: 'We saw the Flemish training school; it has a three-year course while, as you know, in Holland the study would last for another six years at the least. They don't even require you to finish the course before you can apply for a place as an evangelist. What is wanted is the gift of giving popular and attractive lectures and addresses to people, better short and interesting than long and learned. So they require less knowledge of ancient languages and less theological study (though everything one knows is an asset), but they value more highly fitness for practical work and natural faith . . . In short, one must be a popular orator to succeed there. Ces messieurs in Brussels wanted me to come for three months to become better acquainted, but that again would be too expensive, and that must be avoided as far as possible' (Etten, 22 July 1878: 123). Vincent was expected in Brussels in the middle of August 1878. The training school was at Laeken near Brussels. On his first visit to this school he was accompanied by Mr Jones, with whom he had worked in England. Jones had come over from Isleworth to Etten specially for this occasion. Vincent had remained in contact with him (123, 124, 130).

Vincent hoped that after this training he would be in a position to go to work in the south of Belgium, the Walloon part, in the mining area of the Borinage near the French border, just as he had hoped in England (126) to work among the *mineworkers*. The trial period of three months at the Flemish (and thus not French-speaking) training school in Laeken did not mean that Vincent could go on to follow the training (lasting three years) on the same conditions as the Flemish students. Because he did not want to be a burden on his father, he therefore accepted this position as evangelist in the Borinage (Hulsker, 1993, 118). It was his own wish to begin to work there instead of taking the course in Brussels (ibid., 123).

As soon as the trial period of three months was up, he in fact hoped to be appointed there: 'The three months' probation

demanded of me by the Reverend Mr de Jong and the
Reverend Mr Pietersen have almost passed. St Paul was in
Arabia three years before he began to preach, and before he
started on his great missionary journeys and his real work
among the Gentiles. If I could work quietly in such a district
for about three years, always learning and observing, then I
should not come back without having something to say that
was really worth hearing. I say this in all humility and yet with
confidence.

If God wills, and if he spares my life, I would be ready by
about my thirtieth year – beginning with my own unique
training and experience, mastering my work better and being
riper for it than now. I am writing you this again, although we
have already discussed it many a time. There are many little
Protestant communities in the Borinage already, and certainly
schools, also. I wish I could get a position there as an evangelist . . . preaching the gospel to the poor – those who need it
most and for whom it is so well suited – and then devoting
myself to teaching during the week' (Laeken, 15 November
1878, 126). When Vincent had followed this training for three
months, he wrote: 'I spoke with the Reverend Mr de Jong and
Master Bokma: they have told me that I cannot be at the
school on the same conditions as the native Flemish are
allowed to do – I can attend the lessons free of charge if necessary, but this is the only privilege. To stay here longer, I ought
to have greater financial resources than I have, which are non-
existent. So perhaps I shall soon try the Borinage plan. Once
in the country, I shall not soon go back to a big town' (126).

Evangelist in the Borinage

After a trial period of three months, however, initially he was
refused an appointment. On the instigation of his father he
then went on his own account to the Borinage, the mining area
in Belgium. First he lived with the hawker van den Haegen,
to whose children he gave lessons. To begin with he was a

temporary evangelist during December 1878 in Petit-Wasmes, not far from Mons in the Borinage. In January 1879, to his joy, he got a temporary appointment from a missionary society (*Comité d'Evangelisation*) in Brussels as evangelist in the Borinage. The Synodical Committee appointed him evangelist in Wasmes. He served a small community there.

Vincent gives a good description of the atmosphere of life in the coalfield where he worked. He related how he had been down a mine for six hours: 'It was Marcasse, one of the oldest and most dangerous mines in the neighbourhood. It has a bad reputation because many perish in it, either going down or coming up, or through poisoned air, firedamp explosion, water seepage, cave-ins, etc. It is a gloomy place and at first everything around looks dreary and desolate' (129). 'A few days ago it was a remarkable sight watching the miners going home in the white snow in the evening twilight. These people are quite black. When they come out of the dark mines into daylight, they look exactly like chimney sweeps. Their houses are usually small and might better be called huts; they are scattered along the sunken roads, and in the wood, and on the slopes of the hills' (127). Vincent recognized the consequences for the people of the straitened circumstances in which they worked: 'Most of the miners are thin and pale from fever; they look tired and emaciated, weather-beaten and aged before their time. On the whole the women are faded and worn. Around the mine are poor miners' huts, with a few dead trees black from smoke . . .' (129).

Vincent gave lessons in religion and also sermons in the mining district. On the one hand he acted as an evangelist and preacher, on the other hand his pastoral concern for people came out. As for the first: 'I have already spoken in public here several times, in a rather large room especially arranged for religious meetings, as well as at the meetings they hold in the evenings in the miners' cottages, which may best be called Bible classes. Among other things, I spoke about the parable of the mustard seed, the barren fig tree, the man born blind. At

Christmas, of course, about the stable in Bethlehem and peace on earth. If with God's blessing I get a permanent appointment here, I shall be very, very happy' (Petites Wasmes, 26 December 1878, 127). At one particular meeting he chose Acts 16.9 as a text: 'And Paul had a vision in the night: a man from Macedonia stood there and called to him, "Cross over to Macedonia and help us."' According to Vincent people listened to his sermon attentively, 'when I tried to describe what the Macedonian who needed and longed for the comfort of the gospel and for knowledge of the only true God was like. How we must think of him as a labourer with lines of sorrow and suffering and fatigue in his face, without comeliness or splendour, but with an immortal soul – who needed the food that does not perish, God's word. How Jesus Christ is the Master who can comfort and strengthen a man like the Macedonian – a labourer and working man whose life is hard – because he is the great man of sorrows who knows our ills, who was called a carpenter's son though he was the Son of God, who worked for thirty years in a humble carpenter's shop to fulfil God's will. And God wills that in imitation of Christ man should live humbly and go through life not reaching for the sky, but adapting himself to the earth below, learning from the gospel to be meek and simple of heart' (127).

But Vincent was not just content with preaching. He visited the sick, of which there were a great many. 'I have already had occasion to visit some patients, as there are many sick people here. I wrote today to the President of the Committee of Evangelization, asking him if my case could be brought up at the next meeting of the committee' (127).

Vincent had real compassion for those who suffered. He took upon himself the lot of the mineworkers so personally and went so far in his identification with their needs that he gave up his 'comfortable' room in order to show his solidarity with the poor population. He gave away not only money but also his clothes and his bed. He tore his linen in pieces to bind wounds. He only kept the most indispensable clothes. For among his small flock he shared out all that he had, his sparse salary and his clothes. People said that he had a heart of gold. Vincent gave a great deal of money to buy Bibles and New Testaments which he distributed free of charge. His father once had to come to Cuesmes to make him put an end to this distribution of books (I, 228).

He does not write much about the difficulties that he had, except for a remark like this: 'Dear fellow, if I had stayed in Cuesmes a month longer, I should have fallen ill with misery. You must not imagine that I live richly here, for my chief food is dry bread and some potatoes or chestnuts which people sell here on the street corners, but by having a somewhat better room and by occasionally taking a somewhat better meal in a restaurant whenever I can afford it, I shall get on very well. But for almost two years I have had a hard time in the Borinage – it was no pleasure trip' (Brussels, 1 November 1880, 138).

The assessment of Vincent's work as an evangelist

However, Vincent's understanding of the gospel was too radical for the missionary society. They were even so shocked that they removed him from office. Someone from Brussels gave the reasons for his dismissal: 'He didn't stay long. He didn't know how to be submissive. Just as he couldn't cope with his training as a preacher, so he couldn't cope with his training as an evangelist . . . When Master Bokma asked him, "Van Gogh, should this be a dative or an accusative?", he replied, "Sir, I can't tell the difference." When he spoke at a meeting he read out a long passage from a paper – which doesn't go down very well in Flemish groups. It is well known that shortly afterwards he went to Walloon territory and worked among the mineworkers; he gave away all his clothes, so that he didn't go around in trousers and jacket; he slept on a plank' (in one of the newspapers of 12 April 1912, 'Vincent en Meester Bokma', 126a).

It is fascinating to read the verdict of a colleague of Vincent's from a neighbouring place, although it was written fifteen years after the event. This aged preacher M. Bonte, who was preacher in the nearby village of Wasmes from 1878, declared: 'He was the son of a Dutch preacher. I remember his arrival in Pâturages. He was a fair young man of moderate height and with an attractive appearance . . . His French was good and he could speak quite audibly in the religious meetings of the small Protestant group in Wasmes to which he had been appointed.' He went on: 'But our evangelist very soon showed particular feelings about his accommodation: he thought it too luxurious. It shocked his Christian humility; he couldn't bear to be housed so differently from the mineworkers. So he left these people who surrounded him with sympathy and went to live in a little hut. He remained all alone; he had no furniture and it was said that he slept huddled up in the corner of the hearth . . . Faced with the misery which he encountered on his visits, his compassion had driven him to give away almost all his clothes: his money had also gone to the poor and he had kept virtually nothing for himself. His religious feelings were very strong and he wanted to obey the words of Jesus Christ in the most absolute way.

He felt that he had to follow the first Christians, to sacrifice everything that he could do without, and he wanted to divest himself of more than most mine workers to whom he preached the gospel. I might add that Dutch cleanliness in particular was also thrown overboard; soap was given up as a sinful luxury and if our evangelist was not covered with a layer of coal, he usually looked as dirty as the charcoal burners.

He wasn't bothered about outward appearances; he was caught up in his ideal of abstinence; he also showed that his attitude was not to leave things as they were but truly to carry out the ideas that dominated his conscience. While he had no concern for his own welfare, his heart was aroused by the needs of others. He preferred to go to the most unfortunate, the injured, the sick. He spent a long time with them; he was ready to make all these sacrifices to relieve them. His deep sensitivity extended further than human beings. Vincent respected the life of animals, even the least of them. He didn't scorn ugly caterpillars; they were living creatures that one must preserve' (I, 224, 225).

'It is also related that he brought about famous conversions among the Protestants of Wasmes. People still speak of the mineworker whom he visited after an accident that had taken place in the Marcasse coal mine. The man was an alcoholic, an unbeliever and a blasphemer. When Vincent arrived to help him and comfort him, he was received by a bellyful of curses. In particular he was told he was a "chewer of rosaries", as if he was a Catholic priest, but Van Gogh's evangelical tenderness converted the man' (I, 227).

On the occasion of a mine disaster it is said that he rested neither day nor night and gave away the rest of his linen to bandage the wounded (I, 226).

Other witnesses relate: 'An inspector of the *Comité d'Évangélisation* thought that the missionary's excess of zeal was bordering on the scandalous and did not conceal his views from the Wasmes church council. Finally Vincent's father appeared. He travelled from Nuenen to Wasmes, where he found his son sitting on a sack filled with straw, terribly weak and emaciated. Some miners with starving and suffering faces thronged round Vincent . . . The missionary allowed himself to be led away like a child and returned to the lodgings of Mme Denis' (I, 227).

Whatever his 'community' may have thought of him or whatever was the view of his closest 'colleague', the Committee which had appointed him did not want him. The official verdict on him is well known. We learn the reason for his dismissal from a report of the Union of Protestant Churches in Belgium dated 1879–1880: 'The examination which has been made to determine whether to accept the services of a young Dutchman. Mr Vincent van Gogh, who thought that he had been called to evangelize in the Borinage, has not produced the expected results. If the admirable qualities which he showed towards the sick and injured, the dedication and spirit of sacrifice of which he gave many proofs, devoting sleepless nights to them and giving them most of his clothes and linen, had been associated with the gift of the word, indispensable for anyone who is put at the head of a community, then Mr van Gogh would certainly have been a successful evangelist. Doubtless it would not be reasonable to require extraordinary talents of him. But it is certain that the absence of certain qualities can completely ruin the exercise of the prime function of being an evangelist. Unfortunately that was the case with Mr van Gogh. So now that the trial period has passed – some months – one must not think of detaining him longer' (I, 227, 228). Thus the main reason for the dismissal was his lack of a gift of the word.

However, one can ask whether Jansen isn't right when he says: 'Because the missionary society thought that Vincent was interpreting the gospel in too radical a way, he was finally removed from office. Isn't it remarkable that someone who declared himself so truly to be in solidarity with the most exploited people of the nineteenth century should have been removed from office? The history of twentieth-century Christianity also shows that anyone who tries to bring the parable of the Good Samaritan up to date himself becomes extremely vulnerable, and that his vulnerability becomes a threat to the *status quo* of church and society' (Jansen, 193).

After his dismissal as an evangelist Vincent began to work towards his vocation as a painter. But did he also cease to be an evangelist?

3

Van Gogh as a Painter-Evangelist

'Those who had previously gathered around the pulpit now
reverently came to stand round the easel' (Brom, 182).

'From that year on – 1880 – he no longer preached the gospel
through the word but through the image' (Miedema, 37).

In 1879 Vincent was forced to give up his work as an evangelist. Now he began to devote himself entirely to his calling as
an artist. He had to learn the art of painting and drawing. Just
as he had already been much occupied with art before he
became a painter, so as an artist he did not give up his vocation as an evangelist. But he now 'evangelized' in the way of an
artist. Here he was influenced both by the work of other artists
and by the literature that he read intensively. Both helped him
to portray human beings and nature. I shall concentrate in this
chapter above all on the former, the portrayal of other people.

The influence of other artists

Vincent might not have succeeded in following a regular university course to become a preacher – he could not even get
through the preliminary training – but he had taken a 'free
course in the great university of human misery' (Seznec, 131).

In order to express this social concern with suffering
humanity in his drawing and paintings, Vincent was inspired
both by the work of other artists and by literature. As for the
first, he was influenced by reproductions in French, American,
German, Dutch and especially English journals. He cut illustrations out of these journals. *The Graphic* is an example of
this. Already in the time when he was working for the art

dealers Goupil and Co, he was struck by the socially coloured illustrations in *The Graphic* and *The Illustrated London News*. He made a collection of them. Every week he went along the shop windows to look at the most recent numbers. He had almost the complete set of the English journal *The Graphic* (275), as is evident from a letter to van Rappard (R 23) (around 20 January 1883): 'While I was looking them over – during his stay in The Hague – all my memories of London ten years ago came back to me, when I saw them for the first time; they moved me so deeply that I have been thinking about them ever since, for instance Hol's "The Foundling" and Herkomer's "Old Women".'

Vincent made engravings with social subjects after the drawings of recent masters like Hubert Herkomer. He wrote this about them: 'What I value in Herkomer and in other illustrators of *The Graphic* . . . is that they choose subjects that have something noble about them and with a serious sentiment. That must remain, above all, it seems to me.'

Vincent drew inspiration from these drawings.

One of the artists who inspired him from the beginning was the French peasant painter François Millet. Just as his father was the model that he wanted to follow for the first period of his life, when he wanted to become a 'sower of the word' (89, 93), so in the second period he was inspired by 'father' Millet – as is evident for example from 'The Potato Eaters' – when in a certain sense he remained 'sower' and evangelist. Millet continued to preoccupy him from the beginning to the end of his life as a painter. Already in one of his first letters he says of Millet's painting 'The Evening Angelus': 'That is it, that is rich, that is poetry. How I should like to talk to you about art; but now we must write about it often. Admire as much as you can; most people do not admire enough' (London, January 1874, 13). In Saint-Rémy this interest in the peasant painting of Millet returned with force. One might think of all the harvest scenes that he painted at that time. 'The artist has a social mission. Millet realized this' (Seznec, 131).

So Vincent said: 'I consider Millet, not Manet, to be that essentially modern painter who opened a new horizon to many' (355).

The influence of literature

Apart from the influence of the art of others on Vincent van Gogh's work we must also consider the inspiration from literature. Not only was Vincent for a while a rabid reader of the Bible – in Dordrecht, for example, every day (88) – he also read a great many literary works. 'I have a more or less irresistible passion for books,' he wrote (133). Beyond doubt these authors exerted a great influence on his life and work. We know about this in some detail both because Vincent wrote about it, and also because sometimes he depicts books in his paintings with recognizable titles: 'So I have studied quite thoroughly the books within my reach like the Bible, and Michelet's *French Revolution*, and last winter Shakespeare and a bit of Victor Hugo and Dickens, and Harriet Beecher Stowe and recently Aeschylus,' Vincent wrote in Petit-Wasmes (July 1880, 133). In one of his letters to his sister from Paris it is evident how reading particular books could affect him: 'So I, for instance, who can count so many years in my life during which a desire to laugh had utterly disappeared – leaving aside whether this was my own fault or not – I, for instance feel first of all the need of a thoroughly good laugh. I found this in Guy de Maupassant, and there are others – among the older writers Rabelais, among those of the present day Henri Rochefort – in whose works one may find it. Voltaire in *Candide*. If, on the contrary, one wants truth, life as it is, then there are for instance de Goncourt in *Germinie Lacerteux*, *La Fille Elisa*, Zola in *La joie de vivre* and *L'assommoir*, and so many other masterpieces. They paint life as they feel it themselves, and thus they satisfy the need we all feel to be told the truth. The work of the French naturalists, Zola, Flaubert, Guy de Maupassant, de Goncourt, Richepin,

Daudet and Huysmans is magnificent, and one can hardly be said to belong to one's time if one has paid no attention to it. Maupassant's masterpiece is *Bel Ami*; I hope I shall be able to get it for you' (second half of 1887, to Wil van Gogh, W 1). In another letter to the same sister he writes from Saint-Rémy: 'A boundless admiration for de Goncourt, Zola, Flaubert, Maupassant, Huysmans' (W 14).

I shall say more about some of these authors, referring to Vincent's own testimony about them. It clearly indicates what they meant to him.

Van Gogh said that Balzac described society from 1815 to 1848. Zola began where Balzac stopped and went to Sedan, or rather to his day. He therefore called Zola 'Balzac II' (219). Balzac called himself the archaeologist of the social system and the registrar of good and evil in social life (thus Stellingwerff, 35).

– George Eliot analysed 'like Balzac or Zola – but English situations, with an English sentiment' (267).

– Vincent said of Tolstoy, whose *My Religion* he had read, on the basis of an article that he had read about him, that he was enormously occupied with the religion of his people (542. Saint-Rémy, 19 September 1889; W 14).

Vincent read and re-read *Uncle Tom's Cabin* by Harriet Beecher Stowe *with the utmost attention*, also because it had been written by a woman who by her own account wrote the book while she was making soup for her children (W 11). 'This is far from any theology, simply the fact that the poorest little woodcutter or peasant on the heath or miner can have moments of emotion and inspiration which give him a feeling of an eternal home, and of being close to it' (248). The book made him realize that there is still so much slavery in the world (130).

– Vincent read and re-read Charles Dickens' *Christmas Tales* almost every year with similar attention (112). He had an almost complete French edition of Dickens which had been translated under the supervision of Dickens himself (R 30) .'I bought a new sixpenny edition of Dickens's *Christmas Tales* and *Haunted Man* ... I admire everything that Dickens wrote, but I have reread these two "fairy tales" nearly every year since I was a boy and they are new to me again every time ... There is no writer, in my view, who is so much a painter and a sketcher as Dickens' (undated, March 1883; R 30).

– One of the authors whom Vincent van Gogh quotes frequently is Victor Hugo, not least his novel *Les Misérables*: 'It is good to read such a book again, I think, just to keep some feelings and moods alive. Especially love of humanity, and faith in and consciousness of something higher, in short, *quelque chose là-haut*' (277)

– What Vincent finds in the royal dramas of Shakespeare (as in some novelists of our day) 'is that the voices of these people, which in Shakespeare's case reach us from a distance of several centuries, do not seem unfamiliar to us. It is so alive that you think you know them and see them' (597).

The French historian and moralist Jules Michelet (1798–1874), the very anti-clerical professor at the Sorbonne, made the greatest impression on Vincent along with Zola, and was to have a great influence on him in his anti-dogmatism (Kodera, 137). According to Stellingwerff (36), at least in the years 1880–1885 Vincent's morality was largely based on what he had learned from Michelet (about the French Revolution and the 1848 Revolution). Miedema remarks (54) that in the France of his time Michelet did 'pioneering work with his defence of democratic principles and his fight against the Jesuits, driven by the same longing for justice and love, born of faith, that lived in Vincent and with which Michelet in *L'Amour*, starting from the bad and humiliating conditions of marriage and family circumstances, together with unsound views about the significance of the position of women in the family and society, wanted to show how moral liberation was brought about by true love'. Vincent himself wrote: 'For myself I learn much from father Michelet . . . The men and women who may be considered to stand at the head of

modern civilization – for instance, Michelet and Beecher
Stowe, Carlyle and George Eliot and so many others, they call
to us: "O man, whoever you are, with a heart in your body,
help us to found something real, something abiding, something true. Limit yourself to one profession and love one
woman only. Let your profession be a modern one and create
in your wife a free modern soul; deliver her from the terrible
prejudices which chain her. Do not doubt God's help if you do
what God wants you to do, and God wants us in this time to
reform the world by reforming morals, by renewing the light
and the fire of eternal love. By these means you will succeed
and at the same time have a good influence on those around
you, fewer or more, depending on your circumstances." In
my opinion these are the words that Michelet says to us in
general' (160).

Stellingwerff comes to the conclusion that 'literature gave
Vincent van Gogh a view of the century in which he lived. The
past and its spirit became a reality that could be experienced
through the reading of novels' (43). But literature did not take
the place of reality. After mentioning Michelet's book *La
femme, la religion et le prêtre*, Vincent says: 'Books like that
are full of realism, but what is more real than reality itself, and
where is more life than in life itself?' (164).

The multitude that Vincent saw

Inspired by the Bible, the work of other artists, especially
Millet, and what he learned about the situation of human
beings, both men and women (!), in the nineteenth century,
Vincent van Gogh looked with compassion on his needy
fellow men and women. That is evident from the drawings
and paintings that he did and the letters which he wrote about
them from the period in the Borinage, The Hague, Drenthe,
Brabant and France. He was inspired by his Christian
upbringing and practice, and by the models of painters whose
work he sometimes knew only through reproductions.

Many examples could be given of the compassion with which Vincent looked on people – in word and image. Here is just a selection.

– In Laeken he wrote: 'As to the drivers themselves, with their filthy, grimy clothes, they seemed sunk and rooted almost deeper in poverty than that long row, or rather group, of poor people that Master De Groux drew in his "Le Banc des Pauvres". It always strikes me, and it is very peculiar, that when we see the image of unutterable and indescribable desolation – of loneliness, poverty and misery, the end or extreme of all things – the thought of God comes into our minds. At least it does with me, and doesn't Pa also say, "There is no place I like to speak in better than a churchyard, for not only are we all standing on equal ground, we always feel it"' (Laeken, 15 November 1878, 126).

– From the Borinage he wrote: 'Not to mention, as I should have done in the first place, the characteristic and picturesque figures of all kinds of working men, diggers, woodcutters, a servant leading a pair of horses, and sometimes the figure of a woman in a white cap. Even in Courrières there was a mine or pit. I saw the day shift coming up in the twilight, but there were no women in men's clothes as in the Borinage, only miners with tired and miserable faces, blackened by the coal dust, clad in tattered miners' clothes, and one of them in an old soldier's cape . . . Occasionally I earned some crusts of bread along the road in exchange for some drawings I had in my bag' (Cuesmes, 24 September 1880, 136).

– In Etten Vincent drew 'a woman in a white cap, peeling potatoes, a shepherd leaning on his staff, and finally an old, sick farmer sitting on a chair near the hearth with his head in his hands and his elbows on his knees. Diggers, sowers, ploughers, men and women, they are what I must draw continually' (150).

– In The Hague, Vincent sat 'alone in the soup kitchen or in the third-class waiting room or such localities to scribble' (170). There he made a sketch prompted by a poem of

Thomas Hood (1799–1845) in which Hood told 'of a rich lady who cannot sleep at night because when she went out to buy a dress during the day she saw the poor seamstress – pale, consumptive, emaciated – sitting at work in a stuffy room. And now she is conscience-stricken about her wealth, and wakes in fright during the night. In short, it is the figure of a slender, pale woman, restless in the dark night' (185).

So he drew a man by the hearth, the 'almshouse man', i.e. someone who lived in a poorhouse at the cost of the community (195).

In one of his letters he asked Theo whether he remembered the state lottery clerk at the beginning of Spuistraat in The Hague: 'I passed there one rainy morning when a crowd of people stood waiting to get their lottery tickets. The majority were old women and the kind of people of whom one cannot say what they are doing or how they live, but who evidently have a great deal of drudgery and trouble and care in the world. Of course, superficially such a group of people who apparently take so much interest in "today's draw" seems rather ridiculous to you and me, because neither you nor I care in the slightest for the lottery. But that little group of people – their expression of waiting – struck me, and while I sketched it, it took on a larger, deeper significance for me than at first. For it is more significant when one sees in it *the poor and money*. . . The curiosity and the illusion about the lottery seem more or less childish to us – but it becomes serious when one thinks of the contrast between misery and that kind of forlorn effort of the poor wretches to try to save themselves by buying a lottery ticket, paid for with their last pennies, which should have gone on food' (around 1 October 1882, 235; cf. JH, 225).

Vincent drew an almshouse man from the Dutch Reformed Old People's Home at The Hague (236), miner's wives carrying sacks of coal in the snow (241), and two diggers (243). 'Today and yesterday I drew two figures of an old man, sitting with his elbows on his knees and his head in his hands . . . Perhaps I shall also make a lithograph of it. How beautiful

such an old workman is, with his patched bombazine clothes and his bald head' (The Hague, 24 November 1882, 247).

'You may remember that drawing "Worn Out",' Vincent wrote to van Rappard. 'I did it again the other day . . . an old workman sitting lost in thought, his elbows on his knees, and his hands clasping his head (this time with a bald crown) . . . I drew the digger in twelve different poses and I'm still trying to find something better' (R 18).

'You know yourself how beautiful are the numerous figures in repose, which are done so very, very often. They are done more often than figures at work. It's always very tempting to draw a figure at rest; it's very difficult to express action, and in many people's eyes the former effect is more "pleasant" than something else' (251).

He wrote of a watercolour, 'a sketch from life', which he made of a boy and a girl in a soup kitchen, that there was 'perhaps some life in it, and some human sentiment' (272).

'I have a sower – a reaper – a woman at the washtub – a *charbonnière* (a woman miner or charcoal burner) – a seamstress – a digger – a woman with a spade – the almshouse man

– a Bénédicité (grace before a meal) – a fellow with a wheel-barrow full of manure' (277).

Vincent wrote of Millet's digging peasant: 'In the sweat of your brow you shall eat your bread, until you return to the earth' (Genesis 3.19). Although there is no digger in the biblical text, Van Gogh referred to it: 'It is a drawing of a digger – my model was the little old almshouse man whom you know already – his bald head, bent over the black earth, seemed to me to be full of a certain significance, reminiscent, for instance, of "you shall eat your bread in the sweat of your brow"' (277; Van Gogh in Brabant, 62).

'Here in the neighbourhood – The Hague – they dig the potatoes with a short-handled fork, and the digger is kneeling. I imagine that something good might be made of those kneel-ing figures in a flat country in the evening, something that might have a certain mood of devotion; therefore I've studied it closely and already have a man *sticking his fork into the ground*, etc.' (295).

Tralbaut says of a painting of 'mother and child': 'All the lack of pity that there can be in life and that leaves its traces in people's faces is expressed here' (Tralbaut, 1972, 37; cf. JH 356). We can see which theme Vincent dealt with from photographs of work that he took and sent to Theo: 'As you see, the photos are: "Sower", "Potato Diggers", "Peat Cutters". I've had some others made: "Sand Pit", "Burning of Weeds", "Refuse Dump", "Potato Digger", one figure, "Coal Heavers", and now last week at Scheveningen I have been working on "Mending Nets" (Scheveningen fisherwomen) . . . Long rows of diggers – poor people employed by the munici-pality – in front of a patch of sandy ground which must be dug. But it's enormously difficult to make . . .' (301).

In Nuenen Vincent painted weavers and spent time in their huts (355, 358). He wrote of the farm labourers and weavers: 'I don't hear the latter complain, but they have a hard time of it. A weaver who works steadily weaves, say, a piece of sixty metres a week. While he weaves, a woman must spool for him,

that is, supply the shuttles with yarn, so two have to work and to live on it. On that piece of cloth he makes a net profit of, for example, 4.50 guilders a week, and nowadays when he takes it to the manufacturer, he is often told that he cannot take another piece home for a week or two. So not only are wages low but work is pretty scarce too. Consequently there is also something agitated and restless about these people' (Nuenen, around 20 January 1885, 392).

'I have here before me some figures: a woman with a spade, seen from behind; another bending to glean the ears of corn; another seen from the front, her head almost on the ground, digging roots. I've been watching those peasant figures here for more than eighteen months now, and their action, just to catch their character' (416). In the way in which Vincent portrayed stooping women, diggers – there are at least eighty works by Van Gogh in which attention is paid to diggers (*Van Gogh in Brabant*, 162) – sheaf binders, winnowers, reapers, he was often inspired by pictures of Millet. He wrote to his sister Wil: 'Oh Millet, Millet! How he painted humanity and that *quelque chose là-haut* which is familiar and yet solemn' (W 20).

Two examples of pictures in which inspiration from Millet played a role (cf. *Van Gogh en Millet*, 18) are two drawings of workers, one reading the Bible, the other praying before lunch. Vincent quotes words of Millet with approval: 'His peasant is painted with the very earth in which he is sowing' (406).

Old man

Thus during his time in The Hague, Vincent van Gogh also treated religious themes in the narrower sense of the word by depicting men and women at prayer (Tralbaut, 1966, 99). But in fact all his work has a religious component: 'It seems to me a painter's duty to try to put an idea into his work. In this print (he enclosed the illustration) I've tried to express (but I can't do it as well or as strikingly as it is in reality; this is merely a weak reflection in a dark mirror) what seems to me one of the strongest proofs of the existence of *quelque chose là-haut* in which Millet believed, namely the existence of God and eternity – certainly in the infinitely touching expression of such a little old man, of which he himself is perhaps unconscious, when he is sitting so quietly in his corner by the fire. At the same time there is something noble, something great, which cannot be destined for the worms' (248).

Praying and reading the Bible

'I have two more drawings now, one of a man reading the Bible, and the other of a man saying grace before his lunch, which is on the table. Both are certainly done in what might be called an old-fashioned sentiment, they are figures like the little old man with his head in his hands. The Bénédicité is, I think, the best, though they complement each other . . . My intention in these two, and in the first little old man, is one and the same, namely to express the peculiar sentiment of Christmas and the New Year. Both in Holland and in England this is always religious, in fact it is that way everywhere, in Brittany and in Alsace, too. Whether or not one agrees precisely with that form of religious sentiment, it's sincere, a feeling one must respect. And I personally can fully share it and even need it, at least in so far as I have a feeling for such a little old man and a belief in *quelque chose là-haut*, even though I'm not entirely sure how or what it may be. I think it a fascinating saying of Victor Hugo, "religions pass away, but God remains". And there's another fine saying of Gavarni: "what matters is to grasp what will not pass away in what passes away".

One of the things which will not pass away is that *quelque chose là-haut* and belief in God, too, though the forms may change – a change which is just as necessary as the renewal of the leaves in spring. But you will understand from this that it wasn't my intention to pay homage to the form in this drawing, but to show that I highly respect the sentiment of Christmas and New Year. And if it has any sentiment or expression, it is because I feel it myself' (12/18 December 1882, 253; for the works mentioned cf. JH 278, 279, 269, 281).

'Sorrow'

The compassion with which Vincent acted, with which he looked and also spoke so much of his oppressed fellow human beings, emerges above all from his pictures of Sien. Vincent portrayed with great compassion the misery of Sien, whom he had literally looked after by taking her into his house.

Vincent referred to one of Zola's novels in which a certain Mme François appears, who 'lifted poor Florent (a drunkard) into her cart and took him home when he was lying unconscious in the middle of the road where the greengrocers' carts were passing. Although the other greengrocers cried, "Let that drunkard lie, we've no time to pick men up out of the gutter . . ." That figure of Mme François stands out so calmly and nobly and sympathetically all through the book, against the background of Les Halles, in contrast to the brutal egotism of the other women. Look, Theo, I think that Mme François is truly humane; and I have done, and will do, for Sien what I think someone like Mme François would have done for Florent . . . Look here, that humanity is the salt of life; I should not care to live without it' (219).

However, Vincent was all too aware of how he was regarded by his family because of his relations with Sien: 'Do I lower myself by living with the people I draw? Do I lower myself when I go into the houses of labourers and poor people and when I receive them in my studio?' (The Hague, 15/27 April 1882, 190).

His compassion for Sien is evident from his letters. In one to his brother he asked: 'But is it wrong that those human feelings were not extinguished or deadened within me – and that my sorrow awoke within me a need of sympathy for others??? I think not. So *at first* Sien was to me only a fellow creature as lonesome and unhappy as myself. However, as I was not discouraged, I was then just in the mood to be able to give her some practical support, which at the same time helped me to stand fast' (212). Vincent had much sympathy for her: 'It's better for her to be saved than to be ruined . . . I can't say exactly what her expression was, but it was something like a sheep that would say, "If I must be slaughtered, I won't try to defend myself"' (314). 'I pity the woman more than ever, because I see that she's so restless . . . When I think of that neglected character of hers, half or rather entirely ruined – one might say *dragged through the gutter* – then I tell myself, "After all she can't be different from what she is," and I would think myself stupid and conceited if I condemned her in big solemn words' (317).

But despite his devotion, in the end Vincent could not avoid a break with her. Even before his departure for Drenthe, when he had to let her go, he wrote about her to Theo from The Hague: 'Dear brother, if you could know my feelings exactly, how I so to speak spent part of myself on the woman, forgetting everything and just concentrating on saving her, if you could feel exactly my melancholy view of life, which, however, doesn't make me indifferent to it; on the contrary I prefer feeling my sorrow to forgetting it or becoming indifferent – if you could feel exactly how I find my serenity in "*worship* of sorrow" and not in illusions . . . I certainly won't speak much about the woman any more, but I shall continue to think of her very often. From the very first, helping her has been a question of all or nothing. I couldn't give her money to live by herself, I *had to* take her into my house if I wanted to be of any use to her. And in my opinion, the right thing would have been to marry her and take her with me to Drenthe, but I admit that both she herself and the circumstances make that impossible; she isn't nice, she isn't good, but neither am I, and so despite everything there was a serious attachment' (6/7 September 1883, 320).

After Vincent had spent some time in Drenthe and worked there, to begin with her fate still constantly occupied him: 'I often think with melancholy of the woman and the children, if only they were provided for; oh, it's the woman's own fault, one might say, and it would be true, but I am afraid her misfortunes will prove greater than her guilt. I knew from the beginning that her character was spoiled, but I hoped she would improve; and now that I don't see her any more and ponder some things I saw in her, it seems to me more and more that she was too far gone for improvement. And this only increases my feeling of pity, and it becomes a melancholy feeling because it is not in my power to redress it. Theo, when I meet on the heath such a poor woman with a child on her arms or at her breast, my eyes get moist. It reminds me of her, her weakness and her untidiness contribute to making the likeness stronger. *I know that she isn't good,* that I've an absolute right to act as I do, that I *couldn't* stay with her back there, that I really *couldn't* take her with me, that what I did was even sensible and wise, whatever you like; but for all that, it cuts me to the quick when I see such a poor little figure feverish and miserable, and it makes my heart melt inside. How much sadness there is in life, but one must not get melancholy and one must seek distraction in other things, and the right thing is to work; but there are moments when one only finds rest in the conviction that "Misfortune will not spare me either"' (Hoogeveen, around 15 September 1883, 324).

The fresh air and life in Drenthe did Vincent good and strengthened him, but he sighed over Sien: 'Oh, if only the poor woman could have enjoyed it too. I think of her with much tender regret – though my common sense tells me clearly that it's impossible in the circumstances . . . Oh, Theo, if she hadn't had any family she would have behaved so much better. (Sien was drawn back into 'the life' especially by her mother.) Women of her kind are certainly bad, but in the first place they are infinitely, oh, infinitely more to be pitied than condemned; and in the second place they have a certain passion, a certain warmth, which is so truly human that the virtuous people might take them as an example, and I for my part understand Jesus' words when he said to the superficially civilized, the respectable people of his time, "The harlots go *before you*..." ' (Matthew 21.31) ... Bad? Que soit? But who is there that is good in these times? What man feels himself so pure that he can play the judge? Far from it. Delacroix would have understood her, I say, and I sometimes think that God's mercy will understand her even better ... I tell you, brother, I'm not good from a minister's point of view. I know very well that, frankly speaking, prostitutes are bad, but I still feel something human in them which prevents me from having the slightest scruple about associating with them; I see nothing particularly wrong in them. I haven't the slightest regret about any past or present association with them. If our society were pure and well regulated, yes, then they would be seducers; but now, in my opinion, one may consider them more as sisters of charity than as anything else' (326).

Vincent also expressed the compassion indicated by his letters in various paintings that he made of Sien, especial in the drawing – April 1882 – which he himself called 'Sorrow'. As a title he put under it a saying of Michelet: 'How is it possible that on earth there is a woman, alone – forsaken?' (186). This quotation comes from the novel *La Femme* (the sequel to *L'Amour*). For Vincent van Gogh, according to Seznec, Michelet seemed to be an advocate of the women victims of modern society. According to Michelet, the nineteenth century was the century of woman's misery and despair. Men had the task of liberating her from all the slavery that oppressed her.

Vincent said of this drawing 'Sorrow' and another, that of 'The Roots', which he connected with it: 'Now I tried to put the same sentiment into the landscape as I put into the figure:

the convulsive, passionate clinging to the earth, and yet being half torn up by the storm. I wanted to express something of the struggle for life in that pale, slender woman's figure, as well as in the black, gnarled and knotty roots' (The Hague, May 1882, 195).

'The Potato Eaters'

There are some other pictures which can be connected with Vincent's own 'religious' view of the reality of human beings and the world: 'The Potato Eaters', 'Peasant Churchyard' and 'Still Life with Open Bible'. Above all the last two have been connected with Vincent's supposed break with the Christian faith. (I shall be returning to this question in Chapter 5.)

The famous painting 'The Potato Eaters', which Vincent continued to think his best work, was painted in Nuenen. This painting also demonstrates quite clearly the influence that Millet had on Vincent. Vincent thought what was said about Millet's peasants, that they seem to be painted with the earth in which they were sowing seed, to be quite correct: 'When I went to the cottage tonight, I found the people at supper in the light of the small window instead of under the lamp – oh, it was amazingly beautiful' (Nuenen, beginning of May 1885, 405).

'Enclosed you will find two scribblings,' he wrote to his brother Theo, 'of a few studies I made while at the same time again working on those peasants around the dish of potatoes' (399). 'I also wanted to tell you that I'm busy working on the potato eaters. I've got a new canvas and painted new studies of the heads; the hands especially are greatly changed. What I'm trying to do most is to bring *life* into it . . . But you know yourself how many times I've painted these heads! And then I drop in every night to correct some details on the spot' (403). 'I should have liked to send you the picture of the potato eaters on that day – Theo's birthday – but although it's getting on well, it isn't quite finished yet . . . I wanted to emphasize that those people, eating their potatoes in the lamplight, have dug the earth with those very hands that they put in the dish, and so it speaks of manual labour, and how they have honestly earned their food. I wanted to give the impression of a way of life quite different from that of us civilized people. So I'm not at all anxious for everyone to like it or to admire it at once . . .

And it might prove to be a real peasant picture. I know that it is. But those who prefer to see the peasants in their sentimental best may do as they like . . . A peasant is more real in his bombazine clothes in the fields than when he goes to church on Sunday in a kind of dress coat' (404).

'Peasant Churchyard' (Nuenen)

Already before he painted 'Peasant Churchyard', Vincent indicated his intention to paint this theme in his letters: 'I've again heard a great deal (from his father who had visited him in The Hague) about Nuenen, that churchyard with the old crosses. I can't get it out of my head. I hope I shall be able to paint it one day' (234). 'I can't get that churchyard with the wooden crosses out of my mind. Perhaps I shall make studies of it beforehand. I should like to do something in the snow – a peasant's burial or the like' (236). 'Do you know what I some-times long to do? To make a trip to Brabant, I should love to draw the old churchyard at Nuenen . . .' (The Hague, around 22 June 1883, 295). 'I should also like to draw Pa's figure when I draw a peasant's funeral, which I certainly intend to do, though it would be very difficult. Leaving the difference of religious opinion out of the question, the figure of a poor village preacher is to me, in type and character, one of the most sympathetic sights I know, and I should not be true to myself if I didn't try it some day . . . It must not be a portrait of Pa, but rather the type of a poor village preacher on his way to visit the sick . . .' (299)

In any case it must not be inferred from these remarks that in making plans to paint this subject Vincent wanted to express a break with faith. The reason that this is so often claimed lies in the fact that Vincent said something about this painting 'Peasant Cemetery' from Nuenen at the beginning of June 1885 which seems to indicate this. Meanwhile Theo's father, the Revd Theo van Gogh, had died on 26 March 1885 and had been buried in that very churchyard. The graves lay around an old tower which he had said in an earlier letter was about to be pulled down (408). He wrote then: 'I wanted to express how those ruins show that *for ages* the peasants have been laid to rest in the very fields which they dug up when alive – I wanted to express what a simple thing death and burial is, just as simple as the falling of an autumn leaf – just a bit of earth dug up – a wooden cross. The fields around, where the grass of the churchyard ends, beyond the little wall, form a last line against the horizon – like the horizon of the sea. And now those ruins tell me how a faith and a religion mouldered away – strongly founded though they were, but how the life and death of the peasants remain for ever the same, budding and withering regularly, like the grass and the flowers growing there in that churchyard. "Religions pass away, God remains" is a saying of Victor Hugo's, whom they also laid to rest recently – on 12 May 1885 (Nuenen, beginning of June 1885, 411).

'Still Life with Open Bible'

From Nuenen Theo sent Vincent a 'still life with an open . . . Bible bound in leather, against a black background, with a yellow-brown foreground, with a touch of citron yellow. I painted that in one stretch on one day' (Nuenen, end of October 1885, 429). In the next letter he wrote about an enclosure which includes 'a Bible that the people at home gave me for you and that I painted as another still life (430). Seeing that this Bible came from his parent's home, the presupposition is that it was his father's Bible. The Bible lies open, as is evident from the commentary, at Isaiah 53 (in Roman numerals LIII), the famous chapter about the suffering servant of the Lord. In the foreground lies Emile Zola's *La joie de vivre* (The Joy of Life), which had appeared a year earlier.

The compassionate look

'When Jesus saw the multitude he was moved with compassion' (Matthew 9.35). The story of the calling and sending out of the disciples of Jesus begins with these words. The disciples are sent out as apostles or missionaries into the harvest, which is great and calls for many workers.

After 1880, Vincent van Gogh, who at first wanted to be such a worker and indeed became one as an (auxiliary) evangelist and preacher in England and Belgium, remained a labourer in the harvest, though in the style of an artist. As a painter he wanted to bring comfort and light: a sower working for the harvest. Vincent's letters from the first period also repeatedly express concern for human beings. In fact there was no change after 1880 in his purpose to serve humanity (Tralbaut, 90).

Vincent, who in England preached about the 'inner compassion' with which the father looked out from afar for his lost son (80), proves from his drawings, paintings and letters to be moved with the same compassion for the 'multitude' and to remain so. Vincent looked out for 'ordinary people', above all for the suffering. Already in England he expressed his preference for the poor aptly: 'Notre Dame is so splendid in the autumn evening among the chestnut trees. But there is something in Paris even more beautiful than the autumn and the churches, and that is the poor' (75). In a letter from Amsterdam he wrote: 'For who are those in whom one notes signs of some higher life? They are the ones who merit the words, "Labourers, your life is dreary; labourers, you suffer during life; labourers, you are blessed"; they are the ones who bear the signs of "a whole life of struggle and constant work without ever faltering". It's good to try to become like this' (3 April 1878, 121).

From Amsterdam his thoughts again turned to Paris and to the circumstances of people there, 'who for different reasons have strayed from all that is natural and so have lost their real and inner life, and when one also sees so many who live in misery and horror – for in the evening and at night one sees all kinds of black figures wandering about, men as well as women, in whom the terror of the night is personified, and whose misery one must class among the things that have no name in any language' (May 1878, 122).

In Antwerp he wrote: 'But I prefer painting people's eyes to cathedrals, for there is something in the eyes that is not in the cathedral, however solemn and imposing the latter may be – a human soul, be it that of a poor beggar or of a streetwalker, is more interesting to me' (19 December 1885, 441). His letters from the first period before 1880 teem with quotations from the Bible; in the second period he portrays the Bible, once literally, and also he portrays individual direct biblical ideas which will be discussed further in the next chapter. But in his second period as a painter/evangelist his ideas need not be described by the word 'biblical' in the stricter sense to contain a distinctive religious message. The key is that Vincent van Gogh can portray ordinary people as it were with a halo. In his second period Vincent also portrayed the mercy and compassion for his fellow men and women in their wretchedness which he expressed in words and actions in London and in the Borinage: 'I want to paint men and women with that something of the eternal which the halo used to symbolize, and which we seek to convey by the actual radiance and vibration of our colouring,' he wrote in Arles (531). His peasant themes – think of 'The Potato Eaters' – are 'the equivalents of religious themes in art' (Van Uitert, 1983, 80). 'The Potato Eaters' are a kind of holy family. According to Meyer Shapiro the peasant's table stands for the altar and the meal before the sacrament (Shapiro 34, German edition, quoted by Scherer 76, who however does not agree with this interpretation). According to some interpreters the phenomenon of light indicates a religious motif, 'the light as the focal point of the community: a sign of an unearthly power which supports and holds together their community' (Scherer, 77). A modern

Madonna is seen in 'La Berceuse' (Kodera, 81). Of this last painting Vincent himself wrote: 'If I had had the strength to continue, I would have made portraits of saints and holy women from life who would have seemed to belong to another age, and they would be middle-class women of the present day, and yet they would have had something in common with the very primitive Christians' (7/8 September 1889, 605).

From these pictures it is evident above all how Vincent was concerned to depict the underside of society with compassion. Who has drawn such moving figures from behind? Who has depicted an old widower looking at his watch as if he had an appointment (Lawrence)? Who knows like Van Gogh how to give the almshouse man 'a feeling of humanity, of sadness, need of help' (Stellingwerff, 69)? Lawrence associates the hard-working digging and burrowing people with 'the sacraments of work' (Lawrence 51). He gives the people who sit in darkness and whom no one sees (Berthold Brecht) 'a holy aura'. Vincent recognizes Christ as it were in the suffering, poor and hungry, exhausted . . . But what he does above all is to depict sympathetically people on whom he has looked with compassion: tormented, bowed down, and worn out people in the same way as Jesus looked with compassion on the driven and exhausted multitude without a shepherd (Matthew 9.36).

For all that, Van Gogh did not play off word and image against each other: 'There are so many people, above all among our friends, who think that words are unimportant. On the contrary, isn't it just as interesting and even difficult to say something well as to paint something? There is the art of lines and colours, but there is also the art of the word, and always will continue to be' (B[ernard], 4 April 1888).

The 'conversion letter', which has already been mentioned, comes from 1880, the year of that change and the transition to his existence as a painter. I shall quote it, because it immediately makes clear how he could also paint pictures in an unparalleled way in his words:

'There may be a great fire in our soul, yet no one ever comes to warm himself at it, and the passers-by see only a wisp of smoke coming through the chimney, and go on. Look here, now, what must be done? Must one tend that inner fire, seek the power within oneself, wait patiently – with how much impatience – for the hour when somebody will come and sit by it and perhaps stay? Let anyone who believes in God wait for the hour that will come sooner or later . . .

I write somewhat at random whatever comes from my pen. I should be very glad if you could see in me something more than a good-for-nothing. Because there are two kinds of good-for-nothings, who are very different from one another. There is the one who is a good-for-nothing from laziness and from lack of character, from the baseness of his nature. If you like, you may take me as such a person. But there is also the other good-for-nothing, who is a good-for-nothing against his will, who is inwardly consumed by a great longing for action but does nothing, because it is impossible for him to do anything, because he is as it were imprisoned, because he does not possess what he needs to become productive, because circumstances bring him inevitably to that point. Such a man does not always know what he should do, but he instinctively feels, "I am good for something, my life has a purpose after all, I know that I could be quite a different man! How can I be useful, of what service can I be? There is something inside of me, but what is it?" This is quite a different kind of good-for-nothing. If you like, you may take me for such a person.

A caged bird in spring knows quite well that it might serve some end; it is well aware that there is something for it to do, but it cannot do it. What is it? It does not quite remember. Then some vague ideas occur to it, and it says to itself, "The others build their nests and lay their eggs and bring up their little ones"; and then it knocks its head against the bars of the cage. But the cage will not yield, and the bird goes crazy with pain. "It's a good-for-nothing," says another bird in passing, "it's idle." Yet the prisoner lives and does not die; there are no outward signs of what is going on within; its health is good, it is quite cheerful in the sunshine. But then the season of migration comes, and with it attacks of melancholia. "But," say the children who look after the bird in its cage, "it has everything it needs." It looks through the bars at the overcast sky where a thunderstorm is gathering, and deep down it rebels against its fate. "I'm caged, I'm caged, and you tell me I don't want anything, you stupid people! You think I have everything I need! Please give me the *freedom* to be a bird like other birds!" Such a good-for-nothing resembles this good-for-nothing bird. And people are often not in a position to do anything, imprisoned as they are in I know not what horrible, utterly horrible, cage. I know that there is liberation, later liberation: a reputation rightly or wrongly ruined, poverty, fate, adversity – that is what makes people prisoners. You can't always tell what it is that shuts you in, confines you, seems to bury you; nevertheless, I feel intangible barriers, gates, wails. Is all this imagination, fantasy? I don't think so. And then you ask yourself, "My God! Is it for long? Is it for ever? Is it for all eternity?" *Being friends, being brothers, love, that is what opens the prison by some sovereign power,* by some magic force. Without this, one remains in prison. But where affection blossoms again, there life blossoms again.'

4

Van Gogh's Christ

'Once more as he sits here beside me – his English friend Harry Gladwell, the son of an art dealer with whom he worked at Goupil in Paris and with whom he was then living (1875) – I experience the same feeling that drew me to him so often – as if he were a son of the same house and a brother in faith because he loves "the man of sorrows and acquainted with grief" who is our God and in whose teachings and resurrection we believe, whose spirit we seek and whose love we ask for, that it may permeate our lives and that nothing may separate us from it – neither things present nor things to come' (Amsterdam, 7 September 1877, 109).

Vincent was fascinated by the figure of Jesus Christ. Both in his period as an (aspiring) preacher and in his period as a painter – before and after 1880 – the figure of Jesus would not let him go. How did Vincent, even after he was no longer an evangelist or preacher in the narrower sense of the word and had become a painter, think and write about Jesus Christ and portray him?

The discipleship of Christ

As an evangelist Vincent wanted to preach the gospel, and he also put this into practice. In his first period, in addition to reading the Bible he was influenced by the spirituality of John Bunyan and Thomas à Kempis.

At one time Vincent had a Flemish, Dutch, French and Latin edition of *The Imitation of Christ*! 'If I have a chance, I shall send you a French Bible and *L'Imitation de Jésus Christ*. This was probably the favourite book of the lady painted by P. de Champaigne; in the Louvre there is a portrait of her daughter, a nun, also by P. de C.; she has the *Imitation* on the chair beside her' (15 July 1875, 31). Later from Amsterdam he wrote to Theo that he would soon be sending him a Flemish edition of *The Imitation of Christ*: 'a small book which can easily be carried in the pocket' (3 March 1878, 120). Vincent got the Latin edition from the Revd Mr Vos, and he expressed the hope that he would be able to read it in that language (109). 'I'm also copying the whole of the *Imitation of Christ* from a French edition which I borrowed from Uncle Cor; the book is sublime, and the one who wrote it must have been a man after God's own heart. A few days ago such an irresistible longing for that book came over me, perhaps because I so often look at the lithograph after Ruyperez, that I asked Uncle Cor to lend it to me; now I'm copying it in the evening. It means a lot of work, but I've finished most of it, and I know no better way to get it into my head' (108). Later he says about the content of the book: 'Thomas à Kempis's book is remarkable: in it are words so profound and serious that one cannot read them without emotion, almost fear – at least if one reads with a sincere desire for light and truth – the language has an eloquence which wins the heart because it comes from the heart' (108). 'That book by Thomas à Kempis is as beautiful as, for instance, Ary Scheffer's '*Consolator*' – it can be compared to nothing else,' he wrote while still in The Hague (267).

Vincent found Bunyan's *Pilgrim's Progress* 'very worth while' (82), and he made a précis of it (112). He said to Mendes da Costa that Bunyan's book along with the Bible and Thomas à Kempis were far more useful than the study of classical languages (122a). Among the books which Vincent knew, mention can also be made in this connection of Ernest Renan's *Life of Jesus*. That was already the case in the earliest period in London (I, xxiii, 23, 42, 400, 587, 595, 597; W 11).

How much for him art (and artists) continued to be connected with the Bible is evident when in his famous 'conversion letter' he said: 'There is something of Rembrandt in the Gospel, or something of the gospel in Rembrandt . . . And in Bunyan there is Maris or Millet and in Beecher Stowe there is Ary Scheffer' (133).

Vincent initially felt bound up with faith in Jesus Christ as he had received it from home. 'Faith in God is firm in me – it isn't imagination or empty faith. It's the case, it's true, that here is a God who is alive; he is with our parents, and *his eye is also upon us*; and I am sure that he has his eye on us and that we do not wholly belong to ourselves. This God is no other than Christ, of whom we read in our Bible and whose word and history is also deep in your heart' (98). Although there was a clash between Vincent and his father and also with 'official' church Christianity, Jesus remained important for him. In Nuenen he said that he was no friend of contemporary Christianity, but 'the founder was sublime' (378).

In a letter to Theo, after a quotation from Michelet about the development from a 'real satyr' to one who stood before his judges, and in whom, shortly before his death, 'there was something I do not know what, of a god, a ray of light from on high', he continues: 'One sees the same phenomenon in Jesus too: first he was an ordinary carpenter, but raised himself to something else, whatever it may have been, a personality so full of pity, love, goodness, seriousness that one is still attracted by it. Generally a carpenter's apprentice becomes a master carpenter, narrow-minded, dry, miserly, vain; and whatever may be said of Jesus, he had another conception of things from my friend the carpenter of the backyard, who has raised himself to the rank of house owner, and is much vainer and has a higher opinion of himself than Jesus had' (The Hague, July 1883, 306).

That Jesus Christ *continued* to occupy him is evident from a letter to his sister Wil van Gogh. In Paris – by then we are already well into the second period, 1887 – Vincent writes to her: 'Is the Bible enough for us? In these days, I believe, Jesus himself would say to those who sit down in a state of melancholy, "It is not here, it is risen. Why do you seek the living among the dead?" (Luke 24.45,6). If the spoken or written word is to remain the light of the world, then it is our right and our duty to acknowledge that we are living in a period when it should be spoken and written in such a way that – in order to find something equally great, and equally good, and equally original, and equally powerful to revolutionize the whole of society – we may compare it with a clear conscience to the old revolution of the Christians.

I myself am always glad that I have read the Bible more thoroughly than many people nowadays, because it eases my mind somewhat to know that there were once such lofty ideas. But precisely because I think the old things so beautiful, I think the new things beautiful *à plus forte raison. À plus forte raison*, because we can act in our own time, and the past as well as the future concern us only indirectly' (Paris, second half of 1887, W 1).

Christ in the art of others

In his 'evangelist period' Christ *in art* already occupied him. Just as in the first period, so too after 1880 Vincent – of course, one must say – discussed the works of other artists in which Christ was central.

After a visit to his sister in Welwyn, he spoke about the presence in her room of 'Good Friday', 'Christ in the Garden of Olives' and '*Mater Dolorosa*' (18 July 1876, 69). From England he wrote about the famous engravings '*Christus Consolator*' and '*Remunerator*' (70): these last were by Ary Scheffer (1790–1885), a romantic painter of biblical and religious subjects. In a subsequent letter he wrote: 'Thank you, the two engravings – by Ary Scheffer – are hanging over the desk in my little room' (Isleworth, 8 July 1876, 71). In this last letter he also wrote: 'Don't have too many illusions about the freedom I have; I am bound in different ways, some even humiliating, and these will increase in time; but the words written over "*Christus Consolator*", "He has come to proclaim liberty to the captives", are still true today.' In

'La Veillée', oil on canvas, 1889, Rijksmuseum Amsterdam

'Almshouse Man with a
Top Hat and Umbrella
Looking at his Watch',
pencil 1882

'Old Man with his Head in his Hands', litho, 1882

'Peasant Woman Digging, Seen from the Back',
black chalk, 1885

Pietà (after Delacroix), oil on canvas, 1890,
Van Gogh Museum, Amsterdam

Dordrecht he took Theo and his father to the museum where these paintings by Ary Scheffer hung, and he found them 'unforgettable' , especially Scheffer's 'Christ on the Mount of Olives' of 1839 and '*Christus Consolator*' of 1837 (84, 85, cf. Hammacher, 31). Vincent had them hung in his room in Dordrecht. In Amsterdam he expressed his admiration to the engraving by Ary Scheffer, 'The Holy Women at Christ's Tomb' (111). He thanked Theo for sending him '*Christus Consolator*' (116), and a couple of months later wrote: 'Every morning the prints on the wall remind me of you.' Among them he mentions '*Christus Consolator*'.

The person who lived with Vincent in Dordrecht related how later Vincent asked him if he might hang biblical prints on the wall. 'After half an hour the whole room was decorated with biblical scenes and with *Ecce Homos*, and under every head of Christ Van Gogh had written: "Always sorrowful, but always rejoicing"' (IV, 330).

In June 1885 Vincent wrote of a painting by Fritz von Uhde (1848–1911), a German painter of religious themes (Hulsker, 1988, 283): 'I assure you that Uhde's Christ is *particularly* unfortunate, it definitely doesn't work' (Nuenen, beginning of July 1885, 416). Of Uhde's painting 'Let the Children Come to Me', he says: 'I prefer interiors in a bright tone with peasant children, *without* a mystic figure of Christ, as Israëls or Artz paint them, to this one , where one gets a mystic Christ into the bargain . . . My objection to Uhde's picture is that there is a certain coldness in it, like in the new brick houses and schools and the Methodist churches . . . There is after all something consumptive in it, and I think a Corot, a Dupré, a Millet, infinitely healthier in tone' (414). In Antwerp he had seen Rubens' 'Vierge au Perroquet', 'Christ à la Paille' (in the straw) (beginning of January, 332) and he found 'Christ in Purgatory' very attractive.

From The Hague he wrote that he had given Mauve an etching by Nicolas Maes, 'The Stable in Bethlehem', as a present: 'Very good in light and colour, but the expression doesn't work. It's quite wrong. Once I saw this in reality, not of course the birth of Jesus, but the birth of a calf. And I remember the expression exactly. There was a little girl in the stable that night – in the Borinage – a little brown peasant girl with a white nightcap; she had tears of compassion for the poor cow when the beast was in labour and was having great trouble. It was pure, holy, wonderful, beautiful, like a Correggio, a Millet, an Israëls' (181).

The remarks that he was prompted to make by a confinement of Sien's can also be associated with this Christmas scene: 'And though it was only a hospital where she was lying and I was sitting by her, it is always the eternal poetry of Christmas night with the baby in the stable – as the old Dutch painters saw it, and Millet and Breton – a light in the darkness, a star in the dark night' (213). He had the same associations later when he painted the 'Veillée' (cf. JH 1834). 'I've finished the "Veillée",' he wrote in a letter from Saint-Rémy. 'The "Veillée" is in a colour scheme of violets and tender lilacs with the pale lemon of the lamp, then the orange glow of the fire and the man in red ochre' (613). In the 'Veillée' he clearly wanted to get the feeling of 'Christmas night with the child in the stable' (Louis van Tilborgh, 89). 'I should so much like Jo – Theo's wife, who was at that moment expecting a baby – to see the "Veillée",' he wrote (613).

'Christ as artist': Jesus Christ in Vincent van Gogh's art

This last reference to the 'Veillée' already brings us to the question of the way in which Vincent himself depicted Jesus Christ. Vincent van Gogh occupied himself with portraying Jesus Christ above all under the inspiration of the works of particular artists, especially Millet, Delacroix and Rembrandt. In the case of Millet we must think especially of his 'Sower' and the way in which all his life as an artist Vincent was preoccupied with this theme. 'The figure of Christ, as I feel it, has been painted only by Delacroix and Rembrandt . . . and later

Millet painted . . . the teaching of Christ,' Vincent wrote to Bernard (B 8). This letter is worth quoting at greater length, because here it becomes evident how he saw Jesus at a much later time: 'It's a very good thing for you to read the Bible . . . The Bible is Christ, for the Old Testament leads up to this culminating point. Paul and the evangelists occupy the other slope of the sacred mountain . . . But the consolation of that saddening Bible which arouses our despair and our indignation – the consolation which is contained in it, like a kernel in a hard shell, a bitter pulp, is Christ . . . Christ alone – of all the philosophers, Magi, etc. – has affirmed as a principal certainty, eternal life, the infinity of time, the nothingness of death, the necessity and the *raison d'être* of serenity and devotion. He lived serenely, *as a greater artist than all other artists*, despising marble and clay and colour, working in the living flesh. That is to say that this matchless artist, hardly to be conceived of with the blunt instrument of our modern, nervous, stupefied brains, made neither statues nor pictures nor books; he loudly proclaimed that he made . . . *living people*, immortals. That's serious, above all because it's the truth. This great artist didn't write books either: surely Christian literature as a whole would have filled him with indignation, and literary products which would find favour in discerning eyes beside the Gospel of Luke's and the letters of Paul – so simple in their hard and militant form. Though this great artist – Christ – disdained writing books on ideas (sensations), he surely disdained the spoken word much less – particularly the parable (what a sower, what a harvest, what a fig tree!, etc.). And who would dare to tell us that he lied on that day when, scornfully foretelling the collapse of the Roman edifice, he declared, "Heaven and earth shall pass away, but my words shall not pass away." Those spoken words which, like a prodigal *grand seigneur*, he did not even deign to write down, are one of the highest summits – the very highest summit – reached by art, which becomes a creative force there, a pure creative power. These considerations, my dear comrade

Bernard, lead us very far, very far afield; they raise us above
art itself. They make us see the art of creating life, the art of
being immortal and alive at the same time. They are connected
with painting. The patron of painters – Luke, physician,
painter, evangelist – whose symbol is, alas, nothing but an ox,
is there to give us hope. Yet our real and true lives are rather
humble, these lives of us painters, who drag out our existence
under the stupefying yoke of the difficulties of a profession
which can hardly be practised on this thankless planet, on
whose surface "the love of art makes us lose the true love"'
(Arles, end of June 1888: B 8 (11)).

Vincent van Gogh did not just arrive at making his own
pictures of Christ. These emerge above all from the discussion
which he had about them with his painter friends Paul
Gauguin and Emile Bernard. In a letter to Bernard we get
some information about Vincent's images and feelings about
these painters and *their* depictions of Christ. In the autumn
Van Gogh had received some examples of paintings from
them. Bernard sent him photographs of the Annunciation and
the Adoration of the Wise Men, a Christ in Gethsemane and
the bearing of the cross. Gauguin sent Vincent in a letter a
sketch of the garden of Gethsemane (Nordenfalk, 135).

In the letter to Bernard, Vincent mentioned Rembrandt
among the Dutchmen who had painted exceptional Christs:
'And in his case it is hardly like anything whatever done by the
other religious painters. It's metaphysical magic. That is how
Rembrandt has painted angels . . . Rembrandt didn't invent
anything. That angel, that strange Christ, the fact is that he
knew them; he felt them there. Delacroix paints a Christ by
means of the unexpected effect of a bright citron-yellow, a
colourful luminous note which possesses the inexpressible
strangeness and charm of a star in the corner of the firmament.
Rembrandt works with tonal values in the same way as
Delacroix works with colours' (Arles, end July 1888, B 12).

But Vincent van Gogh had some reservations about the way
in which Gauguin and Bernard were occupied with reproduc-

ing the idea of Christ. He told Theo that if he could have seen these studies of 'stars' he would have been able to form an idea of what he was discussing with Gauguin and Bernard (595). Bernard had sent him a painting of Gethsemane in which Judas looked like Gauguin. At the same time he received a sketch of 'Christ in the Garden of Olives', also as a self-portrait of Gauguin. Theo wrote to Vincent that he had seen Bernard's 'Christ in the Garden of Olives': 'A violet Christ with red hair and a yellow angel' (IV, 278; T, 20). The point on which the discussion – or argument – turned, at least what was above all emphasized, was that they had not gone to work looking for authentic images which were faithful to reality: 'Enfin, I have a landscape with olive trees and also a new study of a starry sky (JH 1740, 1731). Although I haven't seen either Gauguin's or Bernard's last canvases, I'm convinced that these two studies I've spoken of are similar in feeling. When you've looked at these two studies for some time, and that of the ivy as well, it will perhaps give you some idea, better than words could, of the things that Gauguin and Bernard and I sometimes used to talk about, and which we've thought about a great deal. It isn't a return to the romantic root of religious ideas, no. Nevertheless, by working in the spirit of Delacroix, more than you might think, by a more deliberate colour and not an imitation of reality we could (seek to express) a countryside purer than the suburbs and cabarets of Paris' (Saint-Rémy, 17/18 June 1889; 595). Vincent said that he did not admire Gauguin's 'Christ in the Garden of Olives', of which he had also been given a sketch. He said of Bernard's reproduction, which he was still to get, that he was afraid that his biblical compositions made him want to do something different. Although he himself had seen women picking and gathering olives at that time, he had found no opportunity to draw them for lack of a model. However, he supposed that Gauguin and Bernard had never seen a real olive tree. Therefore he had never gone along with their biblical interpretations. Certainly he had said that Rembrandt and Delacroix had 'done that amazingly well'. He said that he liked them more than the primitives. 'But stop! I don't want to resume this subject. If I continue to stay here – in the hospital at Saint-Rémy – I shan't try to paint a Christ in the Garden of Olives but the picking of the olives as you still see it, giving the proportions of the human figure in it. Perhaps that would make people think . . .' (November 1889, 614).

Whereas he accused Gauguin and Bernard of not being faithful to truth, he himself wanted to paint *real* olives if he were to paint a Garden of Olives – Gethsemane. He tried to embark on such a theme himself: 'The thing is that this month I've been working in the olive groves, because their "Christ in the Garden", with nothing really observed, has made me furious. Of course, with me there is no question of doing anything biblical – and I've written to Bernard and Gauguin too that I consider it our duty to think, not dream, so that when looking at their work I was astonished at their letting themselves go like that. For Bernard has sent me photographs of his canvases. They can be said to be a sort of dream or nightmare, they're certainly erudite enough – you can see that it is someone who is besotted with the primitives – but frankly the English Pre-Raphaelites did it much better, and then again Puvis and Delacroix, much more healthily than the Pre-Raphaelites' (around 20 November 1889, 614; JH 1853–1857).

But perhaps there was more behind this than just a quarrel over whether or not to paint a real model. Vincent had wrestled with the theme of depicting Christ. That is perhaps the underlying reason for his 'conflict' with his friends. It is striking that in his awareness of having little time and working like one possessed, he destroyed a number of his portrayals of Christ. In Arles Vincent wrote: 'I have scraped off a big painted study, an olive garden, with a figure of Christ in blue and orange, and a yellow angel. A red field, green and blue hills . . . I scraped it off because I tell myself that I must not do figures of that importance without models' (Arles, around 8

July 1888, 505). In a later letter he reported: 'For the second time I've scraped off a study of Christ with the angel in the Garden of Olives. You see, I can see real olives here but I can't, or rather I won't, paint any more without models. But I have the thing in my head with the colours, a starry night, the figure of Christ in blue, the strongest blues possible, and the angel blended citron-yellow. And every shade of violet, from a blood-red purple to grey, in the landscape' (540, JH 1581).

He also wrote to Bernard from Arles: 'I have mercilessly destroyed one important canvas – a "Christ with the Angel in Gethsemane" – and another one representing the poet against a starry sky – although the colour was right – because the form had not been studied beforehand from a model, which is necessary in these cases' (Arles, around 4 October 1888, B 19).

When he was temporarily hospitalized in Saint-Rémy, Vincent van Gogh did make some paintings in which Christ played a role and which he did not destroy. The one who did not want to work without a model portrayed these ideas on the basis of models: after Delacroix a Pietà, and after etchings by Rembrandt 'The Good Samaritan' and 'The Raising of Lazarus'.

We must pause over their influence on Van Gogh's work because they shed light on his (painter's) view of Christ. Vincent called his expression of these works of art a translation and compared his work with the interpretation of a musical work. In copying particular works of art by Millet, Delacroix and Rembrandt, 'colour' was crucial for him: 'If someone plays Beethoven, he adds his personal interpretation. In music, and more especially in singing, the *interpretation* of a composer is something, and it is not a hard and fast rule that only the composer should play his own composition. Very good, and I, mostly because I'm ill at present, am trying to do something to console myself, for my own pleasure. I use the black and white by Delacroix or Millet or something of their work as a motif. And then I improvise colour on it, not, you understand, altogether myself, but searching for memories of *their* pictures – just the memory, "the vague consonance of colours which are at least right in spirit" – that's my interpretation. Many people don't copy, others do. I started on it accidentally, and I find that it teaches me things, and above all it sometimes gives me comfort. And then my brush goes between my fingers as a bow would on the violin, and absolutely for my own pleasure' (607). 'It seems to me that painting from these drawings of Millet's is much more *translating into another language* than copying them' (613). 'Rather it's translating into another language – that of colour – the impressions of light and shade in black and white' (623).

I shall discuss the influence and use of Millet, Delacroix and Rembrandt separately.

'The Sower' and the influence of Millet

Vincent followed Millet as a 'peasant painter'. 'The light came from Christ and in the eyes of Van Gogh the hard existence of the peasants was purified by Christ. Therefore he could also see Millet as an evangelist' *(Van Gogh in Brabant,* 27). One of the ways of finding an answer to the question how Vincent saw Jesus Christ is to pause over his development of the theme of *the sower*. In a sense Van Gogh was occupied with this subject all his life.

To begin with, Vincent wanted to become a 'sower of the word' (89, 93). In one of his letters from Amsterdam he related that one Sunday morning he heard the Revd Eliza Laudrillard preach in the early service on 'Jesus walked in the newly sown field'. 'He made a deep impression on me. In that sermon he also spoke about the parable of the sower, and about the man who cast seed into the ground and slept and rose night and day, and the seed sprang up he knew not how . . .' (12 July 1877, 101). In another letter from Amsterdam Vincent uses the imagery of sowing and reaping:

'Whatever a man sows he will also reap, and he who sows to
the Spirit shall of the Spirit reap life everlasting' (110).

However, Vincent associated his work as a *painter* with the
same image: 'I hope to make as many studies as I can, for that
is the seed which must later produce the drawings' (144). 'I
consider making studies like sowing, and making pictures like
reaping' (233).

For Vincent this imagery of the sower, sowing and harvest-
ing can therefore hardly be dissociated from the symbolic
meaning that it has in the Bible. Here we can recall the image
of the sower from Matthew 13.2–9; Luke 8.4–15 and Mark
4.13–20. As we know, Vincent had a great knowledge of the

Bible. In a letter of 7 September 1877 we hear specifically that together with his English friend Gladwell he had read 'the parable of the sower yesterday evening' (109). In this connection it is interesting to note that around 1877 Vincent gave his teacher of classics in Amsterdam, M. B. Mendes da Costa, a print of J. J. van der Maaten's 'Burial in the Corn'. In the margin Vincent wrote – thus, in da Costa's own words, 'ruining' the reproductions (I, 171) – some biblical quotations, Latin quotations from the Bible, including Mark 4.26–29, the very text on which he had heard the Revd Eliza Laurillard preach: 'And he said, The kingdom of God is as if a man casts seed on the earth and sleeps and rises, night and day, and the seed comes up and grows, he knows not how. The earth itself brings forth fruit: first a grain, then an ear, and then the full grain in the ear. When the fruit is ripe he puts the sickle in to cut, because the harvest time has dawned' (cf. Tusakasa Kodera, 'In het zweet uws aanschins; spitters in Van Gogh's oeuvre', in *Van Gogh in Brabant*, 59, 60). Both the sower and the digger 'are figures loaded with a biblical significance in Van Gogh's work' (*Van Gogh in Brabant,* 137).

In depicting the sower in concrete terms Vincent always drew inspiration from Millet, although he had never seen Millet's famous picture of 'The Sower' in the original. He thought that in Millet's 'Sower' 'there is more soul than in an ordinary sower in the field' (257). Vincent related that in a biography of this 'peasant painter' Jean François Millet by Sensier he had read: 'Formerly I have seen sowers who do not set foot on the prepared ground but throw a handful of grain in the air in the form of a cross. And when he steps on the field he speaks in a low voice incomprehensible texts which sound like a prayer' (Sensier, 1888, 123, 124; quoted from Van Tilborgh, 1988, 157).

Vincent painted more than thirty variants of 'The Sower', quite apart from sketches (Van Tilborgh, 188, 156). As is evident from his letters, drawings and paintings, Vincent was occupied with the theme of the sower in Cuesmes and in the

Borinage (Van Tilborgh, 165). First he made literal copies of it and then in the Hague his own first variations on the theme appeared (257). In Etten he wrote: 'Meanwhile I've started on the Millets. "The Sower" is finished' (144). He interpreted the flock of birds in Millet's paintings by the grains of corn which were sown on the field from the hand of the mower, a translation error (?) which is repeated in one of his painted copies from Saint-Rémy (Van Tilborgh, 1988, 165, 150). He wrote to van Rappard: 'Only after a year or two shall I have gained the ability to do a sower who is sowing; there I agree with you' (Etten, 15 October 1881, R 2). In Nuenen he spoke about Millet's 'Sower' (426).

The first sowers were *literal* copies of Millet's painting: 'If Van Gogh in his Dutch period had remained quite close to Millet's original of "The Sower", after his acquaintance with the Impressionists in Paris the painter in Arles tried to translate the grey original of the French master into a new idiom with the help of a personal, expressive use of colour. In this way he wanted to make his own contribution to modern figurative painting' (Van Tilborgh, 1988, 176). In Arles Vincent painted four sowers with a sun on the horizon and two of the four with a tree in the foreground. In Arles he wrote: 'You can tell from this simple mention of the tonal values that it is a composition in which colour plays a very important part . . . I have been longing to do a sower for such a long time, but the things I've wanted for a long time never come off. And so I'm almost afraid of it. And yet, after Millet and Lhermitte, what still remains to be done is – a sower, in colour and in a large size' (501). Van Gogh interpreted the sower here as a symbol of the infinite. As he wrote in Arles to Bernard: 'A longing for the infinite, of which the sower, the sheaf are the symbols, still charms me' (B 7). We also hear: 'Yesterday and today I worked on the sower, which is done completely differently. The sky is yellow and green, the ground violet and orange. There is certainly a picture of this kind to be painted of this splendid subject, and I hope it will be done some day, either by me or by someone else' (503).

'This is a sketch of the latest canvas I am working on, another sower. An immense citron-yellow disc for the sun. A green-yellow sky with pink clouds. The field violet, the sower and the tree Prussian blue. Size 30 canvas' (Arles, around 25 November 1888, 558a).

In Saint-Rémy Vincent painted the sower after Millet twice more (Stellingwerff, 127, 128).

Vincent van Gogh's paintings of the sower and reaper are also connected with an awareness of his own approaching end. In his cell in the Saint-Rémy asylum Van Gogh painted two almost identical versions of the 'Cornfield with Reaper': 'I'm wrestling with a canvas begun a few days before my sickness, a "reaper"; the study is all yellow, terribly thickly painted, but the subject is fine and simple. For I see in the reaper – a vague figure fighting like a devil in the midst of the heat to get to the end of his task – I see in him the image of death, in the sense that humanity might be the wheat he is reaping. So it is, if you like, the opposite of that sower I tried to do before. But there's nothing sad in this death, it goes its way in broad daylight with a sun flooding everything with a light of pure gold . . . There! The reaper is finished, I think it will be one of those you keep at home – it is an image of death as the great book of nature speaks of it – but what I've sought here is the "almost smiling". It's all yellow, except a line of violet hills, a pale fair yellow. I find it strange that I saw it like this from between the iron bars of a cell' (604).

In the parable of the sower in the Gospels, Christ himself is meant by the sower. Perhaps Vincent did not intend to depict Christ himself in the sower (Scherer), but the painting remains closely connected with the biblical symbolism. Vincent van Gogh depicted vividly growth in nature and in life: 'This picture of the sower gives confidence in the future. The work of the peasant has meaning and he can hope for a good harvest' (Scherer, 90).

The Pietà and Delacroix's 'Good Samaritan'

In contrast to Rembrandt, Vincent van Gogh painted almost no biblical scenes. Perhaps here he was also influenced by Millet, of whom he said that he had been reared in the Bible from his youth and did nothing else but read in it – this also applied *par excellence* to Vincent Van Gogh himself – but seldom if ever made biblical pictures (B 21). Therefore it is important to pause over the few biblical pictures that Vincent did in fact paint, what the occasion was for them and what he meant by them.

One of the other painters admired by Vincent in addition to Millet was Delacroix, who had a great influence on the Impressionists by his clear use of colour. Vincent discussed him with his colleagues, including the Belgian Eugène G. Boch, with whom he had spent a day: 'He likes Delacroix, and we talked a lot about Delacroix yesterday. He even knew the violent cartoon of "Christ in the Ship"' (Arles, 3 September 188, 531; cf. the painting, JH 1574).

'Gauguin and I talked a lot about Delacroix, Rembrandt, etc. Our arguments are terribly electric, sometimes we come out of them with our heads as exhausted as a discharged electric battery. We were utterly bewitched, for as Fromentin says so well: Rembrandt is above all a magician and Delacroix a man of God, of the thunder of God and the lightning, the peace in the name of God' (564; Hulsker 1988, 466).

It is not unusual for a beginner in painting to copy someone else's paintings as practice. Really this is done above all by a painter who still has to learn his craft. Vincent, too, initially followed this custom. But in the last phase of his life he again began to copy not only Millet but also the paintings of others. In Vincent's case, at the end of his life that had to do with the fact that from time to time his sickness forced him to stay indoors; he had a lack of models and so depended on such a procedure.

Certainly it was fortuitous when he began to make copies in

Saint-Rémy. In Saint-Rémy, among other things Vincent had Delacroix's Pietà and 'The Good Samaritan' hanging in his room (590). However, when he dropped a reproduction of Delacroix in the paint, he had to paint it again himself. He mentions this last incident in a letter from which at the same time it emerges what kind of feeling and thoughts occupied him at that time: 'When I realize that here the crises tend to take an absurd religious turn, I should almost venture to think that this even necessitates a return to the North. Don't talk too much about this to the doctor when you see him – but I do not know if this isn't caused by living in these old cloisters so many months, both in Arles hospital and here. In fact I really mustn't live in such an atmosphere, one would be better in the street. I'm not indifferent, and even when suffering, sometimes religious thoughts bring me great consolation. And so this last time during my illness an unfortunate accident happened to me – that lithograph of Delacroix's Pietà along with some other sheets fell into some oil and paint and was ruined. I was very distressed – then in the meantime I have been busy and you will see it one day. I made a copy of it on a size 5 or 6 canvas; I hope it has feeling' (605). Later in the same letter he writes: 'I've talked to her – the wife of the supervisor – sometimes when doing some olive trees behind their little house and she told me than that she didn't believe that I was ill – and indeed you would say the same thing yourself now if you could see me working, my brain so clear and my fingers so sure that I've drawn that Pietà by Delacroix without taking a single measurement, and yet there are those four hands and arms in the foreground in it – gestures and twisted postures not exactly easy or simple' (605).

Of an attempt to make these copies, he wrote: 'I've tried to make a copy of Delacroix's "Good Samaritan"' (Saint-Rémy, 3 May 1890, 632; JH 1972, 1655, 1895, 1973, 1974). A month later we hear that Dr Gachet had told him that it would give him great pleasure if Vincent also made a copy of Delacroix's Pietà for him (Auvers-sur-Oise, 3 June 1890,

638). Vincent painted the subject 'Christ in the Ship' ('La Barque de Christ', or 'Christ sur le Lac de Génésareth') seven times (Hulsker, 1988, 389).

Vincent speaks on various occasions of his *interpretation* or *translation* of these paintings and his perspectives (625). Among other things he mentioned Delacroix's *use of colour*: 'Delacroix had a passion for the two colours which are most condemned, and with most reason, citron-yellow and Prussian blue.' According to Vincent, Delacroix made superb use of them (476). In connection with this he wrote of Delacroix's 'Christ on Lake Gennesaret': 'The problem remains this: the "Christ in the Ship" by Delacroix and Millet's "The Sower " are quite different in execution. The "Christ in the Ship" – I'm speaking of the sketch in blue and green with touches of violet, red and a little citron-yellow for the nimbus, the halo – speaks a symbolic language through colour alone' (503). In a letter from 1884 Vincent spoke about the reproduction of autumn with these two colours: 'Autumn is the contrast of the yellow leaves with violet tones' (372). At yet another place he writes: 'Although copying may be the *old* system, that makes absolutely no difference to me. I'm going to copy the "Good Samaritan", by Delacroix too . . .' (607).

Thus Vincent translated Delacroix's Pietà into colour: Mary in deep blue, the dead Christ in yellow. The reddish-brown beard and green shadows in fact suggest a self-portrait of Vincent (Schapiro, 104). He wrote to his sister Wil about this painting: 'The Delacroix is a Pietà, that is to say the dead Christ with the *Mater Dolorosa*. The exhausted corpse lies on the ground in the entrance of a cave, the hands held before it on the left side, and the woman is behind it. It is the evening after a thunderstorm, and that forlorn figure in blue clothes – the loose clothes are agitated by the wind – is sharply outlined against a sky in which violet clouds with golden edges are floating. She too stretches out her empty arms before her in a large gesture of despair, and one sees her hands, the good strong hands of a working woman. This figure with its streaming clothes is nearly as broad as it is high. And while the face of the dead man is in the shadow, the pale head of the woman stands out clearly against a cloud – a contrast which causes those two heads to seem like one sombre-hued flower and one pale flower, arranged in such a way as mutually to intensify their effect . . . I thought that I should send you a sketch of it in order to give you an idea of what Delacroix is. Please understand that this little copy hasn't the slightest value, whatever the point of view. But you may see from it that Delacroix doesn't draw the features of a *Mater Dolorosa* after the manner of the Roman statues, but that there is on the greyish white countenance the lost, vague look of a person exhausted by anxiety and weeping and waking, rather in the manner of Germaine Lacerteux . . .' (Saint-Rémy, 19 September 1889, W 14).

Rembrandt's 'The Raising of Lazarus'

A couple of months before his death, Vincent van Gogh reproduced the picture of the raising of Lazarus after an etching by Rembrandt – May 1890.

At the beginning of May 1890, Vincent thanks Theo from Saint-Rémy for sending some etchings: 'You've chosen just the ones that I've liked for a long time now: the "David", the "Lazarus", the "Samaritan Woman" and the big etching of the "Wounded"; you've added to them the "Blind Man" and the other very little etching, the last one, so mysterious that I'm afraid of it and don't wish to know what it is: I didn't know it, the little "Goldsmith".

But the "Lazarus"! Early this morning I looked at it and I remembered not only what Charles Blanc said of it but in fact even everything that he didn't say . . . I'm perhaps going to try to work from Rembrandt, I've especially an idea for doing the 'Man at Prayer", in the scale of colour from light yellow to violet' (630; JH 1871, 1804). A day later he wrote again: 'The etchings which you sent me are very fine. On the other side of this page I've scribbled a sketch after a painting I have done of three figures which are in the background of the etching of "Lazarus": the dead man and his two sisters. The cave and the corpse are white-yellow-violet. The woman who takes the napkin away from the face of the resurrected man has a green dress and orange hair, the other has black hair and a gown of striped green and pink. In the background a countryside of blue hills, a yellow sunrise. Thus the combination of colours would itself suggest the same thing that the chiaroscuro of the etching expresses' (Saint-Rémy, 3 May 1890, 632: JH 1972, 1655, 1895, 1975, 1974).

The great etching by Rembrandt to which Vincent referred, 'The Raising of Lazarus', was painted by Rembrandt around 1632. In connection with Vincent's translation of this etching it is instructive to look at Rembrandt's own *other* rendering of the same subject. The figure of Christ, depicted from behind, dominates this etching. Amazement and terror can be read on the faces of the onlookers. However, in an etching from 1642 Rembrandt dealt with the same theme again. In it Jesus' figure is reduced to human proportions. Jesus raises Lazarus to life, no longer with a theatrical but with a calm gesture. The miracle bewilders the bystanders, but does not upset the balance (thus Hidde Hoekstra, Vol.2, 63; cf. JH 1972).

W. A. Visser't Hooft has already drawn attention to the difference between Rembrandt's treatment of biblical themes before and after 1642, the year in which his wife Saskia died. 'Under the influence of baroque art, even Rembrandt in his early years thought that one had to express depictions of Christ in a great and majestic way. One had to be able to recognize immediately in these people the Saviour of the World . . . Many works from the earlier period like the Emmaus of 1629, the Resurrection of Lazarus of 1632, the *Ecce Homo* of 1636 seek to prove the authenticity of his divine mission by the dominating figure or by gesture and look . . .

In later years, however, Rembrandt no longer recognized

this Christ clothed in external glory. The Bible had disclosed to him the mystery of the Messiah and his incognito in the world. Rembrandt had understood that the significance of the incarnation is not the divinization of human nature but the love of God, which humiliates itself to the figure of his creature and even to the figure of the servant. Now he knows . . . that the revelation is not a demonstration of God's power and glory which clearly springs to everyone's eye, but is a descent by God which is understood only through faith' (Visser't Hooft, 24).

Visser't Hooft comments on the first etching – the one used by van Gogh: 'Rembrandt sees only the bodily wonder and brings that out through the theatrical gesture of Jesus and the terrified gesture of the onlookers' (Visser't Hooft, 106). On the other: 'Rembrandt now knows that the true miracle is that "Whoever believes in me shall live, even if he is dead", John 11.25' (Visser't Hooft, 108).

One could say that Vincent also *translated* this 'triumphant Christ' of 1632 in his own way, which to some degree is comparable to Rembrandt's own later treatment of the same theme. But Van Gogh goes even further in his translation.

Certainly it seems to me wrong to say that Rembrandt *replaced* the figure of Jesus by the sun (Kodera, 58). In Rembrandt's etching a source of light is certainly also present, though this is not the sun. In the first instance one could suppose that Vincent omitted the dominant figure of Jesus Christ in the etching from his painting, along with other figures. But at another place in the painting Vincent painted the sun, which symbolically stands for Christ.

5

Van Gogh Bible

I shall not see the stalks again,
nor ever bring in the full sheaves,
but make me believe in the harvest,
for which I serve . . .

A. Roland Holst

In this last chapter I want to consider the question whether Vincent van Gogh may be said to have broken with the Christian faith. Must a question-mark be put against Vincent's Christian faith? Is there continuity or discontinuity between the first and second phases of his life? Did he remain 'only true to his social and religious humanism' (Stellingwerff, *Polemios,* xxi)? Did he despise the God of the scriptures as the God of preachers and did he return to the God in nature? Did he break with his belief in God, and was his idea of God dissolved into belief in the wonder of nature and something higher (ibid., xvi, xxi)? Was the faith that Van Gogh discovered a kind of 'pantheistic version of the old Christian religion: God, or the *quelque chose là-haut*' (Van Tilborgh, *Van Gogh en Millet,* 20)? Is the main theme (e.g. of 'Starry Night') the conflict between religion and nature, between Christian faith and naturalism (Kodera, 148)? Did he want to found a new community, 'the yellow' house, under a new god, the 'sun of the Midi' (Kodera, 148)? Is what Kodera says true: 'What he could do was to built a temple of art on the ruins of his father's church' (165)? Did he opt for nature and naturalism and against Christianity (Kondera, Stellingwerff)? Does the sun take the place of Christ? Does 'father' Millet or 'father' Michelet take place of his own father? Does (French) literature (e.g. Zola) replace the Bible? Is literature 'a substitute' for the Bible (Wiley, 118; Kodera, 53, 75)? Did art come to take the place of religion, or is art itself his religion (Tralbaut, 90)?

A break with Christian faith?

Did Vincent van Gogh, who was so pious in the first period of his life, who wanted to become a preacher and evangelist and indeed did so, turn his back on religion on faith and religion after 1880? Is what is said e.g. of Vincent's 'Still Life with Open Bible' true, that this indicates the ruin of his own faith and religion, and after that did he preach the modern sense of life (*La joie de vivre*, Zola: Stellingwerff, 173, 174, cf. also Graetz, 205)? Must a deliberate opposition between the open Bible and Zola's book be seen in that painting? Did this indicate a world of difference between that of his father and his own (Jean Leymarie, 26; according to Hulsker, 1985, 208)? Does it reflect that *quelque chose là-haut,* Victor Hugo's saying which he repeatedly quotes, the conflict of faith 'in an increasing veneration of the literary naturalism of Zola at the expense of clerical literature' (*Van Gogh in Brabant*, 210)? Is Stellingwerff right when he goes so far as to claim that at the end of his life Vincent van Gogh abandoned his Christian faith? 'In his death mask with cigarette, Vincent van Gogh radically abandons his faith in God and eternal life; he laughs at it. From then on reality is limited to life on this earth in this short time. Van Gogh already experienced the collapse of his body; in Amsterdam he felt weak, wretched, sick, and he lost a number of teeth. In these circumstances Vincent paints what Tralbaut calls this 'scornful scherzo', a product of 'lugubrious scepticism or philosophizing mockery' (Stellingwerff, 93).

The conviction that Vincent had turned away from the Christian religion is also associated with the painting of the churchyard in Nuenen with the old tower ('Peasant Churchyard') and Vincent's own commentary in which he connected the ruin of the church tower with the mouldering of faith and religion (411). According to Kodera the main theme of this last painting is not the ruin of the church itself but the contrast between the ruin of the church tower and the peasant churchyard, that is, 'between the transitoriness of the religions and the eternity of the human cycles' (73, 74). He sees the old church tower as a symbol of the God of the theologians and traditional Christianity (74).

But can one in fact write beside the painting of the Bible and the ruined church and that other 'A Pair of Shoes' (JH 1124): 'God is dead but these shoes live. God is no longer real, but shoes are' (Stellingwerff, 93, 94)?

The suggestion that Van Gogh was initially very religious and gave up religion after 1880, when he began his career as a painter, is already to some degree made in the biographical sketch by the widow of Vincent's brother Theo. Mrs J. van Gogh-Bonger wrote that after being religious in his work and also in his letters in the initial period, Vincent gave this up: 'The biblical texts and religious views, which already become scarce in his letters in the last period, now stop completely' (I, xxvi). Hulsker follows her in this judgment. This is true, I think, in the sense that Vincent bade farewell to a particular form of church religion and turned away from a particular kind of pious style. Vincent distanced himself from a particular kind of faith which he had followed in the past. 'If I repent anything, it is the time when mystical and theological notions induced me to lead too secluded a life. Gradually I have thought better of it' (Etten, December 1881; 164). 'Except for the few years which I can hardly understand myself, when I was confused by religious ideas – a kind of mysticism – leaving that period out of it, I have always lived with a certain warmth' (358). 'But what is the meaning of that standpoint and that religion which the respectable people maintain? Oh, they are perfectly *absurd* things, making society a kind of lunatic asylum, a preposterously topsy-turvy world – oh, that mysticism' (375).

It may be that after 1880 there are no longer so many quotations from the Bible in Vincent's letters as there were before. But it seems to me wrong to say, as Hulsker seems to suggest in his commentary on the edition of Vincent's letters: 'In the summer of 1880 Vincent had discovered art as his calling. We no longer come across religious motifs as in the first letters quoted here – the first 136 letters' (Hulsker, 1988, 42). This last of course is true of the biblical quotations and the pious outbursts, but 'religious motives' do return in a new way, or better, remain present.

Already in his long letter of July 1880 when Vincent 'wrote off' his experiences as an evangelist in the Borinage and accepted his vocation as a painter, he spoke critically about a particular sort of religion: 'You should know that with evangelists it's the same as with artists. There is an old academic school, often detestable, tyrannical . . . Their God is like the God of Shakespeare's drunken Falstaff, "the inside of a church"; indeed by a curious coincidence some of these evangelical (???) gentlemen find themselves with the same point of view on spiritual things as that drunken character' (133).

In my view, Vincent van Gogh did not break with Christian faith but with a particular form of Christianity and opted, explicitly and implicitly, but sufficiently clearly expressed in his paintings and drawings, for another kind of faith which is thoroughly Christian and directly connected with the gospel. Vincent may have abandoned a particular traditional Christianity and 'bourgeois' church, but that does not mean that he gave up the focal point of the gospel, Jesus Christ and Christian faith.

Although Vincent's resignation as an evangelist did not involve him in the 'official church', the break which he made with traditional religion and the 'official church' had above all to do with his painful experiences of love. The conflicts with his father – and his uncle the Revd Mr Stricker, the father of Kee Vos, his relationship with the prostitute Sien and his contact with his neighbour in Nuenen, Mrs Margot Begemann (375).

Above all his vain love for his cousin Kee, about which the family was very concerned, influenced Vincent's view of the clerical church: 'At last the reading of the letter – in which he was told to have no further contact with Kee – was finished. I just felt as if I were in church and, after the clergyman's voice had pranced up and down, had heard him say amen; it left me just as cool as an ordinary sermon . . . It isn't the first time I was unable to resist that feeling of affection, yes, affection and love for those women who are so damned and condemned and despised by the clergymen from the pulpit. I do not damn or condemn them, nor do I despise them. I am almost thirty years old – would you think that I've never felt the need of love? . . . But my feeling for Kee Vos is something quite new and quite different. Without realizing it, she's in a kind of prison. She too is poor and can't do all she wishes, and she feels a sort of resignation; I think that the Jesuitism of clergymen and pious ladies often makes more impression on her than on me – they have no hold on me any longer, just because I have learned to see through some of the tricks. But she believes in them and would not be able to bear it if the system of resignation and sin, and God, and heaven knows what else, proved to be vanity. And she never realizes, I fear, that God perhaps really begins when we say the word with which Multatuli finishes his *Prayer of an Unbeliever*: "O God, there is no God." For me, the God of the ministers is as dead as a doornail. But am I an atheist for all that? The ministers think I am – so be it – but I love, and how could I feel love if I didn't live and others didn't live; and then if we live, there's something mysterious in that. Now call it God or human nature or whatever you like, but there is something which I cannot define systematically, though it is very much alive and very real, and see that is God, or as good as God. And dear me, I love Kee for a thousand reasons, but just because I believe in life and reality, I do not become abstract as I used to be when I had the same thought as Kee seems to have now about God and religion' (164).

The break which came about above all with a particular kind of church Christianity was caused by *the break with his father*. In a letter from The Hague he wrote about a violent scene which took place between him and his father at Christmas 1881 in which his father said that it would be better for him to leave the house. 'Well, he said it so decidedly that I actually left the same day. The real reason was that I didn't go to church, and also said that if going to church was compulsory and if I was *forced* to go, I certainly should never go again out of courtesy, as I had done quite regularly all the time I was in Etten. But, oh, in truth there was much more behind it all, including the whole story of what happened this summer between Kee and me.

I don't remember ever having been in such a rage in my life. I frankly said that I thought their whole system of religion horrible, and just because I'd gone too deeply into those questions during a miserable period in my life I didn't want to think of them any more, and had to keep clear of them as of something fatal.

Was I too angry, too violent? Maybe – but even so, it's settled now, once and for all' (166).

It is again evident from an emotional letter of 14 May 1882 from The Hague how much the rejection by Kee had affected him and the effect it had on his view of faith: 'To express my feelings for Kee, I said resolutely, "She, and no other." And her "no, never never" wasn't strong enough to make me give her up. I still had hope, and my love remained alive, despite this refusal, which I thought was like a piece of ice that would melt. But I could find no rest. The strain became unbearable because she was always silent and I never received a word in reply. Then I went to Amsterdam. There they told me, "When you're in the house, Kee leaves it. She answers, 'Certainly not him,' to your 'she, and no other'; your persistence is *disgusting.*" I put my hand in the flame of the lamp and said, "Let me see her for as long as I can keep my hand in the flame.' But I think that they blew out the lamp and said, *"You will not see her.'* And then I had another conversation with her brother, who said officially or officiously that nothing but *rixdollars* could achieve anything. Officially or officiously I thought that very common, and when I left Amsterdam I had the feeling that I had been at the slave market . . . Now you know I believe in God, I didn't doubt the power of love, but then I felt something like, "My God, my God, why have you forsaken me?" and everything became a blank. I thought, "Have I been deceiving myself? . . . O God, there is no God!"' (193).

Vincent's alienation from his father and the 'bourgeois' and 'fashionable' Christianity was also connected with the negative reaction to his cohabitation with Sien (and plans of Theo to marry, of which the family clearly wasn't informed): 'Really, ministers are the most ungodly people in society and dry materialists. Perhaps not right in the pulpit, but in private matters . . . but coming from Pa and Ma, who ought to be humble and contented with simple things, I think their speaking in that way very wicked, and I feel something like shame at their behaviour . . . You and I also sometimes do things which are perhaps sinful; but for all that, we are not merciless, and we feel pity, and for the very reason that we do not consider ourselves perfect and know how things can happen, we do not revile fallen or frail women as ministers do, as if they themselves were the only ones at fault. And now this woman of yours is, moreover, a fashionable woman from a middle-class family, and I really think Pa's error serious. Suppose there were objections – my opinion is that Pa, because he is a shepherd, ought to urge you on to help her and put up with difficulties for the sake of her preservation. One ought to find comfort from people like Pa when society doesn't give comfort – but they're even worse than ordinary people . . . Their mistake is that they aren't humble and humane enough in this case' (288).

So to a certain degree a break came about between Vincent

and official religion. He gave up the official church and theology. This 'break' certainly means a break with a particular kind of faith. He 'would prefer to die a natural death than to prepare himself through the academy' (137). He regarded 'the whole university, the theological faculty at least, as an inexpressible mess, a breeding place of Pharisaism' (326). He had said to his father: 'The moral and religious systems of ministers and academic views are not worth a thing to me' (169).

But it is going too far to see this alienation and break with his father and a certain kind of bourgeois Christianity as a complete break with Christian faith. He could make a clear distinction between 'bourgeois' Christianity and the 'founder' of Christianity himself. 'I fear for her, that the old religion *will again* benumb and freeze her with that damned icy coldness which *once already,* in the distant past, almost killed her, many years ago. Oh, I am no friend of the present Christianity, although its *founder* was sublime; the present-day Christianity I know only too well. That icy coldness hypnotized even me in my youth, but I've taken my revenge since – how? By worshipping the love which they, the theologians, call *sin,* by respecting a whore, etc., and not respecting many would-be respectable pious ladies. For one group, *woman* is always heresy and devilish. To me it's just the reverse' (378).

However, for Vincent all this clearly did not mean giving up belief in God. 'But reluctantly I am inclined (*porté à*) to believe that the best way to know God is to love him very much' (133). 'It is for him to do the deed' (248). 'To believe in God (that does not mean that you should believe all the sermons of the preachers and the arguments and sophistries of the *"begueles dévotes collet monté"* (pious women with high collars), far from it; to me, to believe in God is to feel that there is a God, not dead or stuffed but alive, urging us with irresistible force to *aimer encore.* That's my opinion' (Etten, 161). 'No fixed idea about God, no abstractions, always on the firm ground of life itself, and only attached to that' (451).

Two fathers: two types of faith?

Just as for the first period of his life his father was the model that Vincent wanted to follow, so in his second period he was inspired by 'father' Jean François Millet, the French peasant painter. Millet served as it were as an 'alternative father' for him – so too Michelet. What did this mean for Vincent's faith and religion?

Millet preoccupied him from the beginning to the end of his life as a painter. Millet's *faith* inspired him. 'Millet, however, is the archetype of a *believer*. He often uses the expression "*foi de charbonnier*", and that expression was already a very old one' (333). Vincent compared a drawing by Millet to a sermon in which art won out over religion: 'As to Millet, he is above all the others the man who has this *rayon blanc* (white light). Millet has a gospel, and I ask you, isn't there a difference between a drawing of his and a good sermon? The sermon becomes black by comparison, even supposing that it is good in itself' (326).

The orientation on this 'new father' came out in a letter which Vincent wrote in Drenthe to his brother Theo: '. . . I see that Millet believed more and more firmly in *quelque chose là-haut*. He spoke of it in a way quite different from, for instance, Pa, for he left it more vague; still, for all that, I see more in Millet's vagueness than in Pa. And I find that same quality of Millet's in Rembrandt, in Corot – in short in the work of many, though I mustn't and can't enlarge on this. The end of things need not be the power to explain them, but basing oneself effectively upon them' (337). 'In my eyes Pa is a man who, when he ought to have had it, did not possess any know-ledge of the intimate life of some great men. What I mean to say is that in my opinion Pa never knew, and does not know now, and never will know, what the soul of modern civilization is.' Vincent then names, among others, Millet, Israëls, Herkomer, Michelet, Hugo, Zola and Balzac. 'For me he is the *rayon noir* (black light). Why isn't he a *rayon blanc*? – This is the only fault that I find in Pa' (339a).

The spiritual break with his own father and the orientation on his new father becomes clear in a letter in which there is plainly an allusion to a previous deep discussion between the two brothers: 'I see two brothers walking about in the Hague . . . One says, "I must maintain a certain status, I must stay in business, I don't think that I shall become a painter." The other says, "I'm getting to be like a dog, I feel that the future will probably make me more ugly and rough, and I foresee that a certain *poverty* will be my fate, but I shall become a painter." So the one – a certain status as an art dealer. The other – poverty and painter . . . I'm not speaking against Pa when I consider his character separately, but I do speak against Pa as soon as I compare him with the great father Millet, for instance. Millet's doctrine is so great that Pa's views appear wretchedly petty by comparison. You think this judgment awful in me – I can't help it – it's my deep conviction, and I make no secret of it, because you confuse Pa's character with Corot's character, for instance . . . I also love Pa, as long as my way in life is not made more difficult by differences of opinion. I *do not* love Pa at the moment when a certain narrow-minded pride prevents a complete and decisive reconciliation, which is so desirable, from being brought about generously and efficaciously . . . I don't attach much value to deathbed reconciliations; I prefer to see them *during life*. I'm quite willing to concede that Pa means well, but I should think it infinitely better if it didn't remain restricted to meaning well and might lead to understanding each other at least some time, though it is very much at the last minute. I'm afraid it will never happen! If only you knew how sad I think this is, if you knew how I mourn over it . . .' (347).

From another letter which was enclosed with the previous one, it became evident how much his opposition is directed against *the system* and how he sees his own upbringing as a *rayon noir*, his father's belief, as compared with *rayon blanc*, the belief of Millet the 'believer': 'Theo, in the past I often quarrelled with Pa, because Pa said dictatorially, "It's like this," and I told him. "Pa, you're contradicting yourself, what you say militates absolutely against what you vaguely feel at the bottom of your heart, even if you don't want to feel it." Theo, I stopped quarrelling with Pa wholly and completely long ago, because it's now clear to me that Pa has never reflected upon certain very important things, and never will reflect upon them, and that he clings to a system and does not reason, nor did he ever, nor will he ever reason on the basis of the bare facts. There are too many who do as he does, so that he always finds certain support and strength in the thought that everyone thinks this about it (primarily all the well-regulated, respectable ministers). But he has no other strength, and it is all built on convention and a system, otherwise it would collapse like any other vanity. Pa doesn't wrestle with the plain truth. But now I'm of the opinion that one is one's own enemy if one doesn't want to think things through, if one doesn't say (especially in one's youth), "Look, I myself I do not want to be sustained by a system; I want to tackle things according to reason and conscience. I listen less to my own father, although he isn't a bad man, although I don't speak about him, than I do to people in whom I see more truth. You see, dear brother, I feel a deep, deep, deep respect for Millet, Corot, Doubigny, Breton, Herkomer, Boughton, Jules Dupré, etc., etc., Israëls – I'm far from confusing myself with *them*. I don't consider myself their equal – no – I say, however conceited or whatever else people may think me – still, "*You* will show me the way and I am ready to follow your example rather than Pa's or some schoolmaster's or whoever else's . . ." In short, dear fellow, neither Pa nor Tersteeg (his boss in the art dealer's in The Hague at the time) has given me other than a spurious tranquillity for my conscience; they haven't liberated me, nor have they ever approved of my desire for

freedom and plain truth and my feeling of ignorance and darkness. Now, left to myself, I haven't attained the light or what I
wanted to do yet, never mind; but by resolutely re-editing *their*
systems I think I have gained a certain hope that my exertions
will not be in vain.

And that, before I close my eyes for ever, I shall see the
rayon blanc. However fierce the struggle in my mind may have
been because I haven't yet found it, I've never regretted saying
that I considered the *rayon noir* the *rayon noir*, and definitely
avoided contesting it – except that one shouldn't quarrel over
it, and if I ever quarrelled over it, it was a mistake . . . What Pa
and Tersteeg tried to force on me as a duty was the spectre of
a duty. What they really said was (though not in so many
words): "Earn money and your life will become straight."
Millet says to me: "Make your life straight (at least try to do
so and wrestle with the naked truth) and even earning money
can be managed, and in this too you will not be dishonest . . ."
But, brother, my very grief over so much proves to me that I
myself have definitely done with the systems in question. I've
suffered from them, but in my heart of hearts I no longer
belong to that side of life . . . As far as religion is concerned, I
find less of it in Pa than in Uncle Jan, for instance, though it
stands to reason that many would say the reverse. I think Pa
the opposite of a man of faith. Well, look here, painting
requires a certain *foi de charbonnier* because one can't prove
at the outset that it will succeed and everyone takes a gloomy
view of it. But Theo, though it may be true that both you and
I begin with as many repressed tears as the figures by
Monteyne and Grollo, at the same time we have a little quiet
hope mixed with all our sadness. In the first years of hard
struggling it may even be a sowing of tears, so be it, but we
shall check them, and in the far distance we may have a little
quiet hope of the harvest . . .' (347).

Vincent shows how much he now sees his upbringing as
something darker than a *'rayon noir'*, over against which
Millet stands as a *'rayon blanc'*. 'Father' Millet comes to take

the place of his physical father as a kind of 'father figure'. Millet, the man of faith, comes to stand higher than his father as a man of faith.

Both the Bible and literature

It is not necessary to take the references to literature in Vincent van Gogh as a counter-instance to the Bible and faith. That is true of both his first and second periods. In the first period, when his inner preoccupation with the Bible is quite plain – in Dordrecht he read it deep into the night, so that he slept over his work the next day (94a) – he refers just as much to literature. Thus both the Bible and literature play a crucial role for Vincent van Gogh from the beginning. In London, in one of his earliest letters he writes to Theo: 'So keep to your own ideas, and if you doubt whether they are right, test them with those of the one who dared to say, "I am the truth," or with those of some human person, Michelet, for instance . . .' (21). Equally, in the first period he can relate in the same breath that he has been busy with Uncle Stricker's catechism and has been thoroughly steeping himself in the paintings of Rembrandt: 'Between times I have worked through the whole story of Christ from a catechism book of Uncle Stricker's and copied the texts; they reminded me of so many pictures by Rembrandt and others' (94). Vincent speaks on the one hand of being increasingly attracted and attached to books of the Bible like the Acts of the Apostles and the life of men like Jules Breton, Jacque, Rembrandt, Bosboom and so many others whom he mentions as a source of thoughts (94). Just as no *absolute* opposition needs to be seen between his father and the painter Millet, so too no absolute opposition needs to be seen between his father and authors like Michelet. In the letter from his first period quoted above, after mentioning the names of Jules Breton, Millet, Jacque, Rembrandt and Bosboom, he says: 'What a resemblance there is between the work and life of Pa and that of those men; I value Pa's higher still' (94). Granted, later he seems to say the opposite: 'When Pa sees me with a French book in my hands by Michelet or Victor Hugo he thinks of thieves and murderers, or of "immorality"; but it's too ridiculous . . . I've often said to Pa, "Just read it, even a few pages of such a book, and you'll be moved by it", but Pa obstinately refuses. Just now, when this love (for Kee Vos) took root in my heart, I reread Michelet's book *L'Amour et la Femme*, and so many things became clear to me that would otherwise have become riddles. I told Pa frankly that in the circumstances I attached more value to Michelet's advice than to his own, if I had to choose which of the two I should follow' (159). Although then in the second period he prefers Michelet above his father, that doesn't mean that he writes of the first: he is concerned with both the Bible and Michelet. Whereas he sees the Bible as eternal and permanent, Michelet, of whose book *L'Amour* he says at one point that it was a 'revelation' and a 'gospel' (20), helps: 'But Michelet gives such amazingly practical and clear hints, so directly applicable to this hurried and feverish modern life in which you and I find ourselves.' He mentioned both Michelet and Harriet Beecher Stowe not as authorities to indicate that the gospel was of no value but as those who 'show how it may be applied in our time, in this our life, by you and me, for instance. Michelet even expresses completely and aloud things which the gospel whispers only the germ of' (161).

How much Vincent loved books and found them important is evident from the frequency with which he depicted them literally, title and all. This clearly also gives a message: 'Whenever we see books as a motif in Van Gogh's paintings, we must regard them as a sign of his own love of literature' (Nordenfalk, 138). In one of his earliest letters he writes about a painting of a woman by P. de Champagne: 'She has *The Imitation of Christ* on the chair beside her' (31). When Vincent later himself made a painting of a woman, 'L'Arlésienne', he painted before her on the table, clearly visible, two of his favourite books: Harriet Beecher Stowe's *Uncle Tom's Cabin* and Charles Dickens *Christmas Tales*. These mustn't be played off against Thomas à Kempis's *Imitation of Christ*, any more than in 'Still Life with Open Bible' Zola's *La joie de vivre* must be played off against the Bible.

Vincent was concerned with another contrast, namely that between word and deed. He was concerned with *acts* of love and not (just empty) words. Speaking about what he calls perhaps the most splendid passage in *Uncle Tom's Cabin*, where the poor slave, knowing that he must die, while he is sitting beside his wife for the last time, remembers the words:

> *Let cares like a wild deluge come*
> *And storms of sorrow fall,*
> *May I but safely reach my home,*
> *My peace, my Lord, my all.*

This is far from theology, simply the fact that the poorest little woodcutter or peasant on the heath or miner can have moments of emotion and inspiration which give him a feeling of an eternal home, and being close to it' (248).

On the one hand Vincent can say: 'I can very well do without God both in my life and in my painting' (531), but that is so to speak qualified when in a letter to Bernard (Arles, end of June 1888, B 9) he writes that 'such hollow words as the Good God' no longer say anything to him (cf. Graetz, 205).

At one point he says, e.g. about the reason for painting books that he plans to 'make light in the darkness' (615). One might think of the bright, yellow (!) copy of Zola's *Joie de vivre*. According to Nordenfalk, by painting books in this way Van Gogh clearly indicated what he wanted to express by the books which he introduced into his paintings: 'He wanted to paint them as sources of light and warmth, in his own existence and that of humanity generally' (143).

Comfort

Although we may speak of continuity in Vincent van Gogh's life, it also proves abundantly clear in the sense that both as evangelist and painter he wanted to communicate to others the comfort that he himself needed. Certainly it may be the case that the comfort that he wants to bring as an artist 'must not be confused with the comfort of the church' (Honnegger, 3, 4), but that is no reason to set the two over against each other.

In a letter from the first period from Dordrecht Vincent could conclude with the words, 'May the thought of Christ as a comforter and of God as a lofty room be with you' (89), but in a letter written later – end of June 1888 – to Bernard, he spoke of 'the comfort of that saddening Bible'. He called Christ the core of this comfort (B 8). In various of his rooms in Isleworth in England (81) and in the Netherlands, in Dordrecht and the Hague (213) he had hung Ary Scheffer's '*Christus Consolator*' (!) on the wall. He had also seen the original in the museum in Dordrecht and called it unforgettable (84; 86; 87a). The work of this religious painter was known in the Protestant Netherlands as 'evangelical Christian' *par excellence* (Van Uitert, 1987, 37 n.5). In Amsterdam, he thanked Theo for sending him a reproduction of that same painting (116). When he was speaking of the ties of all kinds that bound him, he quoted the words that stood above the 'consoling Christ: 'He has come to preach deliverance to prisoners.' He said that this saying was still true today (71).

At one point Vincent tells Theo how he was struck by the words from Acts which Paul spoke on the shore on his farewell: 'God *comforts* the simple' (72). The Bible itself became a great comfort for him. He said to the friend with whom he lived in Dordrecht: 'Oh, G (P. C. Görlitz), the Bible is my comfort, my staff in life. It is the most glorious book that I know and it will be my goal to follow what Jesus brought to people' (IV, 330). Bringing comfort and light was central to his sermon about the Macedonian man from Acts 16.9 which he gave in the Borinage: 'And they listened attentively when I tried to describe what the Macedonian who needed and longed for the comfort of the gospel and for knowledge of the only true God was like . . . How Jesus Christ is the Master who can comfort and strengthen a man like the Macedonian – a labourer and working man whose life is hard – because he is the great man of sorrows . . .' (127).

However, Vincent van Gogh wanted to bring comfort not only as a preacher/evangelist but also as an artist (Jaspers, 157; Stellingwerff, 30). In Arles he said how he wanted to express with a painting something 'as comforting as music' (531). It is striking that he directly follows this quotation with a reference to Ary Scheffer, whose 'Christ the Comforter' he had so admired earlier and about which he now says: 'Portraiture so understood does not become like an Ary Scheffer just because there is a blue sky in the background, as in his St Augustine. For Ary Scheffer is so little of a colourist' (531).

During his sickness religious thoughts gave him great comfort (605). When he was sick in Saint-Rémy and was taken into the asylum, he wrote: 'Very good – and, mostly because I am ill at present, I am trying to do something to comfort myself, for my own pleasure' (607).

One of the paintings which were meant to be comforting was 'La Berceuse' (Van Uitert, 1987, 24). Van Uitert associates that painting with Ary Scheffer's *Christus Consolator* because of the comforting function of both.

It was during Christmas 1888, the time of his first nervous breakdown and the wound to his ear, that he was at work on a canvas 'that places the viewer at the very location of God's incarnation, the intersection of love and creativity'. 'I believe that I have already told you that besides these I have a canvas of a *Berceuse* (portrait of Mrs Roulin, the wife of the postman), the very one I was working on when my illness interrupted me' (28 January 1889, 574). 'I got the idea of painting a picture in such a way that sailors – who are at once children and martyrs – seeing it in the cabin of their Icelandic fishing boat, would feel the old sense of being rocked come over them and remember their own lullabies' (ibid). 'The housewife mother has the end of the cord of the cradle in her hand. There the view is put before the cradle of his childhood.' 'That location was for Vincent the most moving evidence of God's presence, the meeting place of divine vulnerability and the germinating power of love' (Edwards, 83).

As both evangelist and painter Vincent van Gogh wanted to bring comfort and light.

Both darkness and light

One of the indications of the continuity between Vincent's first and second periods can be seen by pausing over the role that light and the symbolism of light play in him. In both periods he continues to speak about the same theme in different ways and to paint it.

Darkness and light. He knew of both in his own life and that of others. He spoke about both. He painted both.

Above all in his first letters we hear repeatedly of his longing for the feast of light, *Christmas*. In a letter from Isleworth he spoke of the coming of winter 'and friendly Christmas': 'Well, the dark days before Christmas are already in sight, and after them lies Christmas, like the kindly light of the houses behind the rocks and the water that beats against them on a dark night. Christmas has always been a bright spot for us, and may it always be so' (113), he wrote from Amsterdam. 'Theo, I so long for Christmas and for home and for you' (115). 'I cannot tell you how I long for Christmas' (116). Sien's admission to hospital called up associations with Christmas night for Vincent (213), and later in 'La Veillée' he could give apt expression to this atmosphere, this sentiment of such a scene (613). However, the days of Christmas were also often crisis periods for him, as e.g. in Etten, because of his marriage proposal to Kee Vos or in Arles because of his conflict with Paul Gauguin. 'Every disaster that befell him took place around the twenty-fifth of December, which was evidently fateful for him' (Tralbaut, 92).

Vincent used the symbol of light when he described going to the pulpit to give his first 'sermon' in Richmond: 'I felt like somebody who, emerging from a dark cave underground, comes back to the friendly daylight' (79). He says this of an experience at a Sunday School in Amsterdam. 'The light in the little Sunday-school room in Barndesteeg is only small, but let me keep it burning' (121) In connection with a Rembrandt etching 'Flight to Egypt by Night', he commented: 'How would a man like Pa, who so often goes long distances, even in the night with a lantern, to visit a sick or dying man, to speak with him about the One whose word is a light even in the night of suffering and agony – how would he feel about Rembrandt's etchings . . . ?' (110; cf. Hoekstra I, 40, 41).

In a letter from Dordrecht, thus still from the first period, he wrote with an evangelical emotion, but at the same time with the eye of a painter referring to the symbolism of light: 'It is good to hold firm to a thought of Christ in all places and circumstances. How difficult the life of the peasants in Brabant is, for instance that of Aerssen (a farm labourer who worked in the manse garden in Zundert)! What is the source of their strength? And those poor women, what supports them in life? Don't you think it is what the artist painted in his "Light of the World"?' (88). When in the same letter he expressed his longing to read the Bible – in this period he read it every day – he gave the reason for it by saying: 'I should like to know it by heart and to view life in the light of that phrase, "Your word is a light to my path and a lamp to my feet"' (88). In his view, what he said about the Bible with reference to Psalm 119 (v. 105, 'Your word is a lamp for my feet and a light for my path', also applied to Thomas à Kempis's book. In Isleworth he called Thomas à Kempis's *Imitation of Christ* 'a glorious book that gives light' (80). He went on to say: 'That is a remarkable

book by Thomas à Kempis; in it are words so profound and
serious that one cannot read them without emotion, almost
fear, at least if one reads with a sincere desire for light and
truth; the language has an eloquence which wins the heart
because it comes from the heart' (108). But did not also in
later years 'the spoken or the written word remain the light of
the world' for Vincent (second half of 1887, W 1)? The symbolism of light played a role in the sermons that he wanted to
give. In Amsterdam he wrote: 'Usually I get up very early in
the morning; when the sun rises over the yard and the workmen come pouring in after a while, the sight from my window
is so beautiful that I wish you were here. Will I have such a
morning to sit and write a sermon on "He makes his sun rise
on the evil and on the good," or "Awake you that sleep, and
Christ will give you light," or, "It is right to praise the Lord in
the early morning and it is good for the eyes to see the sun"?
I hope so. It is as if the sun never shines so beautifully as in
a manse or a church' (103). In one of his letters from
Amsterdam, he wrote: 'Twilight is falling – "blessed twilight",
Dickens called it, and indeed he was right. Blessed twilight,
especially when two or three are gathered in his name and he
is in the midst of them, and blessed is he who knows these
things and does them . . .'

In the same letter Vincent described a drawing by
Rembrandt, the house in Bethany: 'In that room twilight has
fallen; the figure of the Lord, noble and impressive, stands out
serious and dark against the window, through which the
evening twilight is filtering. At Jesus' feet sits Mary, who has
chosen the good part, which shall not be taken away from
her; Martha is in the room busy with something or other, if I
remember correctly: she is stirring the fire, or something like
that. I hope that I don't forget either that drawing or what it
seems to say to me: "I am the light of the world: whoever
follows me shall not walk in darkness but have the light of
life" . . .The light of the gospel preached to the poor in the
kingdom of my Father shining like a light on a candlestick on

all who are in the house . . .' (110). In Amsterdam, where he wrestled with his classical languages until late in the evening, his uncle Jan, he related, had forbidden him to work so late. He then continues: 'Still, I keep in mind the words under the etching by Rembrandt: *In medio noctis vim suam lux exerit* (in the middle of the night, the light diffuses its strength)' (112).

It is also fascinating to note how in connection with his work as an *evangelist* among mine workers who above all have to work in the dark, Vincent was attracted by the symbolism of light. At Laeken in Belgium he wrote how in England he had first sought involvement as an evangelist in the coal mines: 'But they put me off, saying that I had to be at least twenty-five years old. You know how one of the roots or foundations, not only of the gospel but of the whole Bible, is "Light that rises in the darkness". *From darkness to light.* Well, who needs this most, who will be receptive to it? Experience has shown that the people who walk in darkness, in the centre of the earth, like the miners in the black coal mines, for instance, are very much impressed by the words of the gospel and believe them too' (126). Vincent noted from a geography book 'how this miner with a helmet and little lamp to guide him through the darkness entrusts himself to God, who sees his labour and protects him, his wife and his children' (126). There is an inscription in Durham Cathedral, in the middle of a coalfield: 'This commemorates before God the miners of this province and those who work in darkness and danger in the mines today.' That is what Vincent did. As an evangelist he wanted to bring the light of the gospel to miners working in the darkness.

But also as an *artist* he wanted to bring not only comfort but light. In the works from the Dutch period you can see, says Miedema, 'what he meant by the *rayon noir*'. If the Dutch period still stood wholly under the sign of the *rayon noir*, the French period was dominated by the *rayon blanc*', 'a burning stream of pure sunlight' (67, 68). In one of his letters to Theo, in which he speaks profoundly about Theo's future, he says: 'I see *everything* against painting except fatality; I see everything *for* Paris *except* fatality. Fatality, in which with an unutterable feeling I see God. That is the *rayon blanc*, and has the last word; what is not good through and through is not good at all and will not last, an even the *rayon noir* will not remain' (337).

To understand what Vincent meant with the images of light, we must consider the way he dealt with *nature*. He had a penetrating eye for the nature around him. That applies above all to the places where he painted. 'When you – Theo – say in your last letter "What a mystery nature is," I quite agree with you. Life in the abstract is already an enigma. Reality makes it an enigma within the enigma, and who are we to solve it? However, we ourselves are an atom of that universe which makes us wonder: Where does it go, to the devil or God? *Pourtant le soleil se lève* (yet the sun rises), as Victor Hugo says (242). In Drenthe he wrote: 'That is an important thing, I think, for in such natural surroundings, things can be roused in a disposition, things which would otherwise never have been awakened' (337). 'What life I think best, oh, without the least shadow of a doubt it is a life consisting of long years of converse with nature in the country – and *quelque chose là-haut* – inconceivable, "awfully unnameable" – for it is impossible to find a name for that which is higher than nature. Be a peasant – be, if it could be considered possible nowadays, a village minister or a schoolmaster, be – and in my opinion this ought to be thought of first, the present times being what they are – a painter, and as a human being, after a number of years living in the country and of having a handicraft, as a human being you will in the course of these years gradually become something better and deeper in the end' (339a). 'The laws of the colours are unutterably beautiful, just because they are *not accidental*. In the same way that people nowadays no longer believe in fantastic miracles, no longer believe in a God who capriciously and despotically jumps from one thing to another, but begin to feel more respect and admiration for and faith in nature' (371). In Arles, where he was occupied par excellence with the depiction of light and the *quelque chose là-haut*, God, he wrote: 'Victor Hugo says that God is a darkening lighthouse, and in that case we are certainly passing through that eclipse now' (around 29 September, 543). 'Van Gogh's innate religious feeling reached its climax in a strong longing to transcend the limits of material reality in order to achieve a spiritual unity with *quelque chose là-haut* . . . His early religious upbringing had taught him to discover in nature the stimulants to arouse people's innate religious feelings' (Murray, 87). Vincent was intensely preoccupied with nature and its portrayal. He saw the possibility of expressing God in nature by referring to the peasant painter Millet (Murray, 81). 'In Van Gogh this higher power had a direct expression in the symbol of the sun. Vincent's capacity for direct experience in nature allowed him to depict the natural phenomenon as a direct representative of the divine' (Scherer 122).

Vincent tried to paint the light in countless ways through *suns* or *sunflowers* and the *stars*.

In his last paintings Vincent tried more than any other painter before him to depict light. Countless paintings show the sun above landscapes. Here the colour *yellow* is particularly striking. He uses this colour above all to depict the light which so influenced him in Provence. It is important to understand Van Gogh's language of colours. He had a special predilection for yellow. 'How lovely yellow is,' he exclaimed in Arles (522). This colour speaks its own language: 'Here nature is so *extraordinary* beautiful. Everywhere and all over the vault of heaven is a radiant blue, and the sun sheds a light of pale sulphur, and it is as soft and as lovely as the combination of heavenly blues and yellow in the canvases of a Van der Meer of Delft' (539). Yellow was the colour for Vincent, the colour of light as it was for Delacroix, whose theory of colours he studied. Yellow stood for light, for the sun, for life itself (Takashina, 416). Nor is it by chance that many books – espe-

cially by French novelists like Zola – were depicted in yellow
and so contained a clear message.

In connection with the significance that the sun was to have
for Vincent in his period in Provence in southern France, it
is perhaps interesting here to quote a letter from his initial
period in Paris – 14 October 1875. He recalled in it that his
father had once written to him: 'Don't forget the story of
Icarus, who wanted to fly to the sun and, having arrived at a
certain height, lost his wings and dropped into the sea.' . . .
'But let us persevere, *above all let us have patience; those who
believe do not hasten*. Still, there is a difference between our
longing to become real Christians and that of Icarus to fly to
the sun' (43).

In the sun Vincent symbolically depicted God, in Victor
Hugo's words the *quelque chose là-haut*.

Reference can be made in this connection to his painting
'Starry Night'. 'I must also do a starry night, with cypresses,
or perhaps above all, a field of ripe corn; there are some
wonderful nights here,' he wrote to Theo (474). He also wrote
in a letter to Bernard that he had tried to make a such a painting (B 3). 'At last I have a landscape with olive trees and also a
new study of a starry sky' (595, JH 1731; cf. Kodera, 146–8).
In connection with this theme of stars one might refer to an
early letter from England which says: 'I have copied a few of
the psalms for you; perhaps you would like to read them one
of these days.' The psalms are 25, 91, 121 and in addition the
hymns 'A Voice is Heard', *'The Light of Stars'* (my italics) and
'As pants the heart'. In the same letter he quotes Longfellow:
'I see the lights of the village gleam through the rain and
the mist, and a felling of sadness comes o'er me, that my soul
cannot resist' (75). In a letter from Amsterdam Vincent
describes the atmosphere on the wharf where he was living:
'At night there is also a beautiful view of the wharf; everything
is dead quiet then and the lamps are burning and the *starry sky*
(my italics) is over it all: "When all sounds cease, God's voice
is heard, under the stars"' (100).

According to Murray, Vincent van Gogh's innate religious feelings are now manifested completely in the wish to achieve complete harmony not only with earthly nature but with the whole cosmos – a drive towards the *quelque chose là-haut* which he was finally able to express in his famous 'Starry Night' of 1889 (Murray, 78). Graetz sees in 'Starry Night' (JH 1731), in which Vincent van Gogh portrayed the top of the tower of a Dutch church in a Provençal landscape (Kodera 64), the fulfilment of Vincent's longing in the sower for the *rayon blanc*. 'His starry sky is completely lit up with rays of light.' Graetz points out that the houses in the village of the painting 'Starry Night' seem to radiate light as a reflection as it were from the ray from above, the light of love, with the church as the only exception. This recalls the 'icy chill' about which Vincent speaks in his letters (348, 378). Graetz does not think that the light from the houses and the church is fortuitous (cf. 103, 121, 330, 643). Although Vincent himself said, 'It is not a return to romantic or religious idea, no' (595), Graetz asks himself whether the striking choice of 'Starry Night' as a religious painting cannot mean that the church, too, seeks light in a dark drive from within (Graetz, 213).

When Vincent tried to paint Christ, it was connected with his approaching end. Here attention must be paid above all to the symbolic language which he used in his paintings. For him *cypresses* and the *olive orchard* – for the depiction of Gethsamene – are realistic symbols. He sets the sunflower over against the cypress (Stellingwerff, 128, 139). 'When I had done those sunflowers, I looked for the contrast and yet the equivalent, and I said – that's the cypress' (625). He saw the sunflower as the flower of the *day* and the cypress as the tree of the *night*. Fear about life is clearly expressed both in the cypress, as Vincent painted it, and in the olive orchard. When Vincent wrote about his fear, he often used the word Gethsemane. In the Garden of Olives Jesus became fearful and an angel had to comfort him. As we have seen, Vincent had

objections to the way in which his painter friends Gauguin
and Bernard depicted the scene, as if they had never seen a real
olive tree. As long as he was in the asylum, Vincent himself did
not try to paint a Christ in the garden of Olives (614). In a
letter to Bernard, Vincent wrote: 'I am telling you about these
two canvases, especially about the first one, to remind you
that one can try to give an impression of anguish without
aiming straight at the historical Garden of Gethsemane; that
it isn't necessary to portray the characters of the Sermon on
the Mount to produce a consoling and gentle motif. Oh,
undoubtedly it's wise and proper to be moved by the Bible,
but modern reality has got such a hold on us that, even when
we attempt to reconstruct the ancient days in our thoughts
abstractly, the minor events of our lives tear us away from our
meditations, and our own adventures thrust us back into our
personal sensations: joy, boredom, suffering, anger or a smile.
The Bible! The Bible! Millet, having been brought up on it
from infancy, did nothing but read that book! And yet he
never, or hardly ever, painted biblical pictures. Corot has
done a "Mount of Olives", with Christ and the evening star,
sublime; in his works one feels Homer, Aeschylus, Sophocles,
as well as the gospel sometimes, yet how discreet it is and
how much all possible modern sensations, common to us all,
predominate . . .' (B 21)

Lövgren concludes from Vincent's objection to his two
painter friends: 'With sarcastic clarity these lines of Van Gogh
disclose suffering and disappointment, when neither Theo nor
his critical friends understood the subtle symbolic message,
the modern religious allegory of his "Starry Night". He understood his feelings by bitterly asserting that he was now
working on the Garden of Olives, his own personal, eternal
Gethsemane' (Lövgren 153, 154).

But Vincent's symbolic language is interpreted wrongly if it
is thought that for him nature and naturalism now replaced
God and religion, or the Bible is to be identified with the
darkness and is to be replaced by the light of literature or the

sun, and the sun takes the place of Christ or his personal Gethsemane the place of Christ's Gethsemane.

In Vincent van Gogh the light of nature *does not replace* the light that he discovered earlier in the Bible. Certainly it is true, as Miedema rightly says, that Vincent van Gogh 'experiences his love of nature and evaluates it differently from before. It is none other than his religious feeling. But it is precisely an expression of it. In nature he discovers God's creative power. His tie to nature means his tie to God. Earlier he had repressed this sense' (Miedema, 50). The burnt-out candle in 'Still Life with Open Bible' does not suggest that for him the light of the Bible is quenched and that the light of Zola – depicted in yellow – now shines alone for him and replaces that of the Bible. Could not the quenched candle stand for the death, six months earlier, of his father, whose Bible it is that he depicts (Lawrence, 67; Takashima, 411)?

No, the Bible is not written off by Vincent van Gogh. It is not by chance that the Bible in this painting lies open at Isaiah 53! In it appear the words: 'He was despised and rejected by men; a man of sorrows and acquainted with grief, and as one from whom men hide their faces he was despised and we esteemed him not' (Isaiah 53.3), words which Vincent quotes (in part) in English in a letter. Vincent, more than any other, knew what sorrow was, both the sorrow in his own life and above all the suffering and sorrow of others.

One of the hymns which he liked and quoted at length in an early letter runs:

Of in sorrow and in woe,
Onward Christians, onward go.
Fight the fight, maintain the strife,
Strengthened with the bread of life.

Let not sorrow dim your eye,
Soon shall ev'ry tear be dry,
Let not fear your course impede,
Great your strength if great your need! (41).

Vincent is very familiar with the chapter about the suffering servant of the Lord. In his sermon he described the Macedonian man (Acts 16.9) who called to Paul in a dream, 'come over and help us', 'as a worker with features of pain and suffering and weariness on his face without comeliness or splendour' (I, 88–91).

In 'Still Life with Open Bible', alongside his father's Bible open at Isaiah 53 Vincent painted Zola's book *La joie de vivre*. Like books elsewhere, this last functions as a focus of light (*foyer de lumière*) (615). With this expression Van Gogh clearly indicated what he meant by his books in his painting. 'He wanted to portray these as a source of light and warmth in his own existence and in that of humankind generally' (Nordenfalk, 143). But if he depicts Zola's novel painted in yellow, it is inconceivable that in so doing he overlooked the passage at which this Bible lies open and what this means.

On the contrary, to think that for van Gogh literature takes the place of the Bible would be completely wrong. For van Gogh, literature did not take the place of the Bible. On 23 November 1881 he wrote to Theo from Etten: 'Take Michelet and Beecher Stowe: they don't say that the gospel is no longer any use but they lead us to understand how applicable it is to this our time, this our life, for example for you and to me, just to mention some people' (161). In a letter to his sister Wil from Paris in the summer or autumn of 1887, he wrote: 'If, on the contrary, one wants truth, life as it is, then there are for instance de Goncourt in *Germinie Lacerteux, La Fille Elisa,* Zola in *La joie de vivre* and *L'assommoir,* and so many other masterpieces. They paint life as they feel it themselves, and thus they satisfy the need we all feel to be told the truth. The work of the French naturalists, Zola, Flaubert, Guy de Maupassant, de Goncourt, Richepin, Daudet and Huysmans is magnificent, and one can hardly be said to belong to one's time if one has paid no attention to it. Maupassant's masterpiece is *Bel Ami*; I hope I shall be able to get it for you.' 'Is the Bible enough for us? In these days, I believe, Jesus himself would say to those who sit down in a state of melancholy, "It is not here, it is risen. Why do you seek the living among the dead?" (Luke 24.45,6). If the spoken or written word is to remain the light of the world, then it is our right and our duty to acknowledge that we are living in a period when it should be spoken and written in such a way that – in order to find something equally great, and equally good, and equally original, and equally powerful to revolutionize the whole of society – we may compare it with a clear conscience to the old revolution of the Christians.

I myself am always glad that I have read the Bible more thoroughly than many people nowadays, because it eases my mind somewhat to know that there were once such lofty ideas. But precisely because I think the old things so beautiful, I think the new things beautiful *à plus forte raison*. *À plus forte raison*, because we can act in our own time, and the past as well as the future concern us only indirectly' (W 1).

In 'Still Life with Open Bible' there is a reference to the story of the suffering servant of the Lord, which has always been applied to the suffering of Jesus by the church. Zola's book puts the story of a certain Pauline next to that of Isaiah (53). Vincent chose Zola's novel because it communicated the story of the Suffering Servant in modern garb. Important novels expound the truths of the Bible for a contemporary audience. 'Vincent saw both the Servant in Isaiah and Pauline Quenu as incarnations of renunciation, sacrifice, and charity. But it was fitting that Zola expressed the Servant mission for a new age in the form of a new body, a joyful young girl, and projected its hope into the future in the form of the child she vowed to raise in the midst of darkness and death' (Edwards, 49, 50, 51). It has been pointed out that it looks as if Van Gogh is referring to v.20 (xx) of Isaiah 53, and in fact the chapter has only twelve verses. This could have been a mistake, but Vincent 'might have been intimating that the story of the Suffering Servant continues to be written' (ibid., 48).

Always before and after 1880 Vincent had an eye for suffering humankind, his own suffering and the suffering of others, men and women. It cannot be fortuitous that Vincent himself wrote the title 'Sorrow' under one of the drawings of Sien. Was she not for him, and did not he paint her as, a kind of woman 'of sorrows'?

Miedema remarks on the much later painting of the dead Christ, after Delacroix's Pietà, that Van Gogh had depicted Mary and her dead son in an infinitely deeper and more moving way than Delacroix ever could. 'She experienced that the prophecy of Isaiah 53 had been fulfilled in her own son' (Miedema, 73).

In my view, 'Still Life with Open Bible' means that Vincent wanted to say different things at the same time. He is alluding on the one hand explicitly to the gloomy and dark suffering of which he was aware as an evangelist and which he also depicted in this and other paintings as a painter and drawer, and on the other hand wanted to bear witness to redemption, to the light, to the joy of life (Zola, *La joie de vivre*), to nature, to flowering and flowers. Thus in a comparable way in the dead Christ in the arms of Mary and the risen Lazarus – in both portraits one can discover the features of Vincent's own face – suffering figures are depicted and salvation announced (Schapiro, 104).

The sun (above the sower)! And the sunflowers

Kodera has a good quotation from the Revd Eliza Laurillard, the preacher whom Vincent once heard preaching in Amsterdam (101, 101a, 110). He wrote about *sunflowers*: 'Therefore in the soul of a poet the thought can arise that God, the Lord, is a sun. But then we must know that the appearance of this sun radiates our spirit and our heart, as we wish the shining of the sun in nature to bring light and joy into our dwelling, and life and fertility to our garden. Yes, we wish our disposition to be like the sunflower, always turning to the Great Light fully to receive the rays of the sun which it sends down' (*Geen dag zonder God*, Amsterdam 1869, 170, quoted by Kodera, 71). Although it is not certain that Vincent knew this passage, it can be applied to his understanding of the symbolism of light: 'Van Gogh saw in the "glorious sun" the climax of what he sought with a burning heart. The sun which rose on good and evil was beyond doubt for him the symbol for God. Not as for St Francis the "noble sister", but the ocean of fire into which one cannot stare without being blinded' (Honnegger, 8, 10).

The sun as a symbol for God and for Christ, not the sun that replaces Christ as, has been suggested in the interpretation of the raising of Lazarus. Not the sun in place of Christ, but *Christ as sun*! Vincent van Gogh, who in the first period of his life so longed for the celebration of the feast of light, the feast of Christmas, does not let Christ be displaced by the sun in his painting. Didn't the early church soon resort to the same image of Christ as sun, when the date of Christmas was moved from 6 January to 25 December, the feast of the invincible sun? At that time the church had no difficulty in welcoming the light of Christ in that festival, the sun of righteousness of which Malachi speaks (4.2). 'Behold salvation!' Only in the Easter mystery 'which as sun has illuminated the underworld and on Easter morning has risen shining as a sun,' writes Julius Firmicius Maternus in the fourth century (*De Errore profanorum religionum*, 22).

Darkness and light

Didn't Vincent also know 'the dark night of the soul', to use the expression of the mystics? He depicted this night as it were in one of his last paintings, 'Wheatfield under Troubled Skies with Crows'. Although his brush was almost falling out of his hands, he painted this with other paintings: 'There are vast fields of wheat under troubled skies, and I didn't need to go out of my way to try to express sadness and extreme loneliness' (649; according to Hulsker, 1985, 476, 478, however, these words do not relate to this particular painting).

Isn't it significant that in the last phase of his life Vincent went almost crazy in his attempt to depict light? In his last letter, which he had written and which was found on his body when he was dead, he wrote: 'Well, my work, I'm risking my life for it and my reason has half foundered because of it' (652). Isn't that experience of going crazy in wanting to attain the light like the experience of the great mystics? In her introduction to *The Desert Fathers,* Helen Waddell writes: 'Gauguin like any desert fanatic left his Paris banking house and his comfortable wife, and watched his small son starve and himself died in nakedness and ecstasy because he had discovered paint as the desert discovered God. Van Gogh went mad in struggling to paint light . . . A man must follow his star. We do not grudge it that these should have left wife and children and lands and reason for the flick of a needle on the speedometer or "a still life of a pair of old shoes". The only field of research in which a man may make no sacrifices, under pain of being called a fanatic, is God' (Waddell, 29).

Vincent van Gogh was and remained to the end of his life a witness to that light!

Christology

This brings me to the nature of Vincent van Gogh's 'theology' or 'christology', if one may use such a heavy word. In his dissertation on Van Gogh, Stellingwerff has emphasized that gap that there is said to be between the early and later Van Gogh. In Van Gogh's theology he misses 'soteriology', the doctrine of salvation. In his view, in the mourning of the dead Christ there is still no question of his resurrection (Stellingwerff, 131). In the raising of Lazarus Vincent is said to have left out Christ, who was in the Rembrandt etching, and added the sun as a symbol of life-giving force, to express in this way the comfort of the helping man, the comfort of nature and the warm sun (132). In the portrayal of the Good Samaritan Vincent is said to have been more concerned with the notion of human help than with *Christian* mercy, in which forgiveness is central. In the Garden of Olives which Vincent paints Stellingwerff finds more images of Vincent's own anguish in life – which is certainly also the case – than the depiction of Gethsemane in which Christ begged and prayed for forgiveness of guilt and the sin of the world. In the Pietà, Vincent mourns the dead Christ who was a good man and a great artist (168). In the raising of Lazarus, Vincent is said to say of the sun: 'behold the way, the truth and life' (178). Stellingwerf asserts that in the Pietà we must see an identification of Vincent with the dead Christ. He says that this must be interpreted humanistically in the spirit of Renan: human need and human help. 'There are no images of biblical salvation through the atonement by Christ.' 'Under the influence of Renan, in the long run Vincent formed his own life of Jesus, radically modern and with a humanistic socialistic tinge' (18). The numerous biblical texts which Vincent van Gogh still cites 'may seem orthodox, but in reality his insight is closer to modern liberal Christianity and against the background shows radical and sometimes also socialist tendencies' (29). He says that Vincent's letter from the Amsterdam period about 'honest' men is more humanistic than Christian (121). Stellingwerff sees a basic humanistic motif at work in Vincent van Gogh: 'The motif of the sower, the grain and the reaper tells us that Vincent sees life as a process of growing and dying, a natural process' (178). He speaks of a transition to 'humanism' in Van Gogh, which he means as a negative qualification which stands over against the basic *biblical* motif: 'In Vincent van Gogh reality proves to be governed by the basic humanistic motif which drove him, just as also reality . . . in Rembrandt van Rijn proves to be determined by the basic biblical motif' (179). For instance, he sees the potato eaters standing *over against* the 'holy family'. 'In Rembrandt there was the happy family, the family in which the life redeemed by Christ flourishes. In Vincent we find a family which through hard work tries to dominate the earth in order to obtain food and a poverty-stricken existence. Here there is an effort in an elemental way to attain a human existence' (Stellingwerff 172).

Such an assessment can be made only on a particular *dogmatic* presupposition about the content of the Christian faith and what is central or must be central in it. A great deal of this interpretation of Vincent van Gogh can be rejected. It seems to me possible to arrive at a far more ecumenical interpretation of Van Gogh's religious views in the second period.

In order to be able to evaluate this judgment and express a view on Vincent's theology it is important first to look at Vincent's religious background. From van Gogh's remarks from the first period it is clear that he was an adherent of an undogmatic form of Christianity. 'Vincent and Theo did not have a Calvinist upbringing. Their father belonged to the Gronigen tendency in the Dutch Reformed Church; at that time that was the moderate tendency in the Dutch Reformed Church' (IV, 324 n.3). This tendency may have had an influence on Vincent through his father. The 'Groningen school' stood between the two extremes of orthodoxy on the one hand and the modern tendency on the other. Vincent's grandfather had studied with the representative of this last tendency, Prof. Dr J. H. Scholten in Leiden. Vincent's father studied theology in Utrecht, where the training as such was hostile to both directions (Tralbaut, 103,104). The Groningen school preached a humanistic Christianity. In its view Christianity was not about doctrines, not about a teaching presented by Jesus. Revelation is to be found in Jesus himself, in his mission, his person, his history. The goal of God's upbringing was humanity. The Groningen tendency did not accept the eternal divinity of Christ, rejected the so-called doctrine of two natures and denied the divinity of Christ and the Trinity. The seriousness of sin as a break with God, the lostness of human beings and God's wrath were toned down, and with this also redemption through doing satisfaction to God's law. The emphasis was put on human feelings, upbringing and constantly increasing sanctification. Basically the foundations of the Groningen school were humanistic by nature. It was critical of the Bible, of which the Gospels were thought to be the most important part. There was antipathy to a creed and a desire for one church above divisions of faith (Tralbaut, 1–6; Kodera, 31: *Christelijke Encyclopedie* (second edition), s.v. 'Groninger School').

In some respects it could be said that Vincent van Gogh's views tended in this direction, although one would have to be careful not to label him too quickly as belonging to such a tendency. From his youth upwards he disagreed with church statements. So he was clearly not brought up in this way. He stood above the divisions of the church. Someone who lived with Vincent in his Dordrecht period was told by Van Gogh after his frequent visits to various churches: 'In every church I see God, and whether the minister or the priest preaches, it is the same to me; God isn't there in dogma, but in the spirit of the gospel and the spirit I find in all churches' (IV, 331). To begin with, his religion was above all influenced by the typical Dutch tendency of the *devotio moderna* of Thomas à Kempis. For a while he also admired John Bunyan. The Baptist Charles Spurgeon was at one time one of his favourite writers (I, 113; IV, 330). In England he regretted having missed the famous evangelists Moody and Sankey. Vincent loved 'the old, old story'. In Ramsgate he noted that there was such a longing for religion among the people in the big cites: 'Many a worker in a factory or shop has had a distinctive, beautiful, pious child-hood. But city life sometimes takes away the "early dew of morning". Still, the longing for the "old, old story" remains: whatever is at the bottom of the heart stays there' (66). Vincent van Gogh had no objection whatsoever to working in England first for a Congregationalist and then for a Methodist preacher. Everything indicates that he attached no importance to dogmatic hair-splitting. But also much later – at the end of September 1888 – he could write to his friend Bernard: 'I profoundly despise regulations, institutions, etc.; in short, what I am looking for is different from dogmas, which, far from settling things, only give rise to endless disputes' (B 18). This anti-dogmatic attitude is also associated with the influence of Jules Michelet (Kodera, 137), but all his activities both before and after 1880 expressed it. It has rightly been said: 'It was not the doctrine of salvation through faith in Christ and Christ alone which dominated Vincent's thought but rather the spirit of the story of the gospel – love, humility, compassion and the self-sacrifice of Jesus, the friend of publicans and sinners' (Lawrence 25). Karl Jaspers is right when he says (as it were in a summary): 'Already strongly religious in his youth, to the end in all that he did he continued to be borne up by a religious feeling without the church or dogmatics' (Jaspers, 140). According to Jaspers' summary, Vincent:

– As an *art dealer* in the Goupil business failed to achieve what was required of him because he put the value of art, the quality of the objects, above the interest of the business.

– As a *teacher* in England failed because in this profession alien things were required of him.

– As a *theologian* failed because the long study kept him away from the sense of bringing the gospel to people and because 'he regarded the whole university, at least as far as theology was concerned, as an unspeakable swindle, as a school for training in Pharisaism' (Jaspers, 140).

Vincent van Gogh did not give up his Christian faith in his second period, but his faith was transformed. His 'theology' became much more comprehensive, indeed 'Catholic' than was usually the case in his pietistic Protestant milieu. He was aware of the social context, although perhaps it is arguable whether he was aware of the political context in which he lived. It may be true that he makes no mention in his letters of the hardness of the mine owners, or of the social unrest among the population which was to break out in 1885; he mentions once in a letter of 1879 (130) that there were strikes (Hammacher, 12). It may be that we do not notice that he followed the international events of his days (Stellingwerff, 25). Perhaps his sermons come close to calling for resignation: 'give poor creatures peace with existence on earth' is how Mendes da Costa describes Vincent's intention in Amsterdam (170). Certainly, 'through his religious crisis and his first social failure he became aware of the workers and the poor in the world capitals. In Paris, in London and later in the Borinage he came into contact with the social question of the nineteenth century' (Stellingwerff, 25). Later he was to write to his sister about this period: 'And yet – you know it – within ten or fifteen years that whole edifice of the national religion collapsed, and – the socialists are still there, and will be there for a long time to come, although neither you nor I are very much addicted to either tendency' (W 4; Stellingwerff, 170). 'He did not become a socialist or a communist, but we do see a combination of religious depth, socialist sentiment and pictorial expression' (Stellingwerff, 30). 'Vincent's work is not simply an expression of his own feelings but at the same time an expression of compassion for the world and people,' Stellingwerff rightly remarks (58).

His awareness of the social context also extended to *nature*. In the first period Vincent was already, perhaps in contrast to Thomas à Kempis, aware of the world around him and nature. In his Dutch period he painted the earth in Drenthe and Brabant: the potato eaters, who worked on this earth and whom he painted with the colours of the earth from which they lived. That awareness of nature becomes even stronger in his French period: the Midi with its sun, sunflowers, blossoming trees and fields. He was also prompted to this by the influence of Japanese art. Vincent learned from these Japanese an attention to detail. He experienced a lucidity which he felt to be a kind of grace ('I feel extremely clearly that it has nothing to do with me'), and 'has a marked need for religion, in the sense of the Japanese religion of nature'. 'If we study Japanese art, we see a man who is undoubtedly wise, philosophical and intelligent, who spends his time doing what?

Studying the distance between the earth and the moon? No. Studying Bismarck's policy? No. He studies a single blade of grass. But this blade of grass leads him to draw every plant and then the seasons, the wide aspects of the countryside, then animals, then the human figure. So he passes his life, and life is too short to do the whole. Now isn't it almost a true religion which these simple Japanese teach us, who live in nature as though they themselves were flowers? And you cannot study Japanese art, it seems to me, without becoming much more aware and happier, and without being brought back to nature in spite of our upbringing and our work in a world of convention' (542).

But Vincent's eye for nature must not be dismissed as 'naturalism' or 'pantheism', or interpreted as a sign that he had exchanged Christian faith for a 'natural religion'. Rather, it must be understood as a glimpse of the comprehensiveness of his Christian theology. He was increasingly open also to nature and creation. He had as it were a 'creation theology'. Vincent did not speak unequivocally: 'A feeling, even a keen one, for the beauties of nature is not the same as a religious feeling, though I think these two stand in close relation to each other,' he wrote in Paris (17 September 1875, 38). 'Was nature as beautiful as he saw it? Was not this extreme beauty and charm a demonic power of attraction through which a person is drawn away from God and at best arrives at a suspicious pantheism? All these theological views and notions belonged to the sphere of the *rayon noir*. From now on he could no longer give up this bond with nature, turn his back on it, but by means of his art bore witness to the divine forces that he discovered in it, not in a superficial glorification, not dominated by false romanticism or by decadent atheism, but prompted by a passionate longing for truth, which will not stop at the external appearances of things, but seeks to penetrate to the deepest depth' (Miedema 50, 51).

Certainly Van Gogh does not seem to have had the same kind of christology or theology as his church surroundings; he even had one which differs from his later Christian critics. Here a phenomenon described by M. D. Chenu takes its revenge: 'The greatest tragedy in the theology of the last three centuries has been the separation of the theologian from the poet, the dancer, the musician, the painter, the dramatist, the actor, the filmmaker' (quoted by Matthew Fox, 180). In this connection it is interesting to note that Vincent himself explicitly spoke of Jesus Christ as an 'artist'. In 1888 he still wrote about Christ as *'l'artiste plus grand que tous les artistes'*, who tried to make people immortal and whose words form an artistic high-point: 'one of the highest summits – the very highest summit – reached by art' (Arles, end June 1888, B 8).

Here it is not a question of judging the Christian content of Vincent van Gogh's letters and works of art on the basis of one particular theological conception in which a particular form of soteriology is regarded as the criterion. In this connection it is perhaps worth quoting a remark by Matthew Fox which could apply to Vincent's own talk of Jesus as an 'artist': 'Jesus chose to act as an artist. This was a deliberate choice on the part of Jesus, namely to speak in parables, and that was a powerfully creative choice. It is specifically Christian in many respects. Docetic and christolatrous spiritualities have nothing to say about this significant choice of Jesus the artist' (Matthew Fox, 239). Wouldn't Vincent van Gogh, who was fond of the parables – in England (106, 127, 138) – have been able to recognize his own intentions in the words of the poem: 'It is all a parable of a more than earthly mystery?'

After 1880 Vincent van Gogh had not abandoned his faith as clearly as it seems from his later letters, but it had changed from that of his original milieu. Vincent van Gogh's 'christology' was more that of the Gospels and the parables than that of Paul. His 'christology' was not so much that of the West, where soteriology in the sense of Christ's redemptive suffering and death is so central, but one which stood closer to Eastern Orthodoxy, where salvation (and thus soteriology) is indeed confessed, but more in terms of the victory of life over death, of light over darkness.

Van Gogh Bible: 'a kind of Bible'

Van Gogh's pursuit of his vocation as a painter in 1880 did not mean a radical or absolute break with his Christian faith and religion. Although it cannot be denied that Vincent broke with much 'bourgeois' Christianity, against the background of the whole history of his life and works it can be said that he was not only an evangelist in this first period, but in the second period too as an artist remained an evangelist, albeit in a quite distinctive way. What Vincent says on one occasion about Rembrandt, namely that 'there is Rembrandt in the gospel and the gospel in Rembrandt' (133), in my view also applies to van Gogh himself. In his period as an evangelist he was already quite clearly the rising artist, and as an artist he remained an evangelist.

When in the winter of 1879 Vincent took the decision to become an artist, 'that only meant the choice of art as a way to attain God and to bear witness to God, above the way of the religious apostolate which he had hitherto followed' (Vanbesselaere, 74). Perhaps after 1880 Vincent van Gogh had given up a particular form of 'pietistic' faith, but his faith was thoroughly *transformed,* as can be said of Rembrandt after 1642. Vincent maintained not a conventional faith but humane behaviour towards Sien (Scherer, 121), human compassion more than fashionable virtue (326). On Mendes da Costa's own account, Vincent did not give the *Imitation of Christ* to Mendes da Costa to convert him, but to show him 'all that is human' in it (I, 170); he was concerned with 'humanity as the salt of life' (219). He was concerned with a Christianity of action, more with the Gospels and the parables than with dogma. He was not so much concerned with an either-or as with a both-and. He was concerned with both the Bible and literature, both his father and 'father' Millet or

Michelet. Certainly the latter transformed the former. Vincent van Gogh knew both sorrow and joy, darkness and light.

In him the human must not be played off against the Christian, but the human must be seen as the best expression of the Christian. Therefore the paintings of ordinary people, above all suffering people, could take on a 'sacred aura' and do not stand over against the potato eaters, but are to be regarded as a holy family.

Thus it should be possible, as is done with the art works of Rembrandt, to compile as it were a Van Gogh Bible from his works. In the case of Rembrandt, of course, that was simple, because Rembrandt had painted numerous biblical pictures. Of course in the first place the paintings of biblical figures would be candidates for such a Van Gogh Bible: the Good Samaritan, the raising of Lazarus, the Pietà or finally the picture of the sower, or also those in which the Bible is literally the subject or theme. Also in this connection one could mention what he wrote about painting a scene from the Old Testament, the burial of Sarah (97), or Elijah in the wilderness 'with a stormy sky, and in the foreground a few thorn bushes. It is nothing special, but I see it all so vividly before me, and I think that at such moments I could speak about it enthusiastically – may it be given me to do so later on' (101). But Miedema was right when he wrote: 'it was not Van Gogh's purpose to illustrate the Bible, but to express the life of faith to which the Bible bears witness through his art' (Miedema, 73).

As it were a Van Gogh Bible could be made with many drawings and paintings by Vincent of ordinary people – the postman, the midwife, toiling peasant men and women: 'a kind of Bible', to use the expression which Vincent himself applied to the illustrations like those in *The Graphic*. Vincent did not want so much to depict Jesus Christ; he had a certain awe of that: 'Isn't Renan's Christ a thousand times more comforting than so many *papier mâché* Christs that they serve up to you in the Duval establishments called Protestant,

Roman Catholic or something-or-other churches?' (587)
Vincent recognized Christ above all anonymously in the
suffering children of men. 'Rather than illustrating the
Gospels or reproducing biblical episodes – something that
Millet rarely did – it is enough to show the suffering of ordinary people, the ordinary people of today; instead of trying to
reconstruct the biblical past through imagination, one must
relate oneself to the misery of the present time' (Seznec, 131).

Vincent van Gogh portrayed anonymous Christs with
moving compassion. And he bore witness to the point of going
mad to how the darkness is overcome by the light of the sun,
the symbol of Christ, and of God.

Bibliography

For the letters of Van Gogh I have made use of the following editions:

Verzamelde Brieven van Vincent Willem van Gogh. Edited with a commentary by his sister-in-law J. van Gogh-Bonger, January 1914. Supplemented and expanded by Dr V. W. van Gogh, 1953. New edition with the collaboration of the Vincent van Gogh Foundation and Uitgeverij B. V. 't Lanthuys, Amsterdam and Antwerpen ⁵1973. (This work is in two volumes comprising four parts. Where references are not to the standard numbering of the letters, they are to the pagination of the parts.) For the English text, reference has been made to the three-volume edition of *The Complete Letters of Vincent van Gogh*, Thames and Hudson 1958. There is an attractive selection of letters by Van Gogh, *The Letters of Vincent van Gogh*, Penguin Books 1997.

See also: Jan Hulsker, *Van Gogh en zijn weg; het complete werk,* Amsterdam 1983 (abbreviated JH)

Jan Hulsker, *Vincent Van Gogh; Een leven in brieven. Keuze, inleiding en toelichting,* Amsterdam ⁴1988. I have sometimes made use of the translations from the French and the datings of the letters.

Van Gogh in Brabant. Drawings and paintings from Etten and Nuenen, Zwolle 1988

Les sources d'inspiration de Vincent van Gogh; Gravures, estampes, Iivres, lettres. Documents du peintre (Expositions 31 janvier–5 mars, Institut Néerlandais), 1972

Other relevant books are:

K. G. Boon, *Rembrandt de etser*, Amsterdam 1963

Gerard Brom, *Schilderkunst en litteratuur in de 19e eeuw*, Utrecht and Antwerp 1959

Ton de Brouwer, *Van Gogh en Nuenen*, Venlo 1984

M. Buchmann, Die Farben bei van Gogh, 1948 (dissertation)

E. H. Cossee, 'Vincent van Gogh en kerkelijk Dordrecht', in *Kwartaal en teken van Dordrecht* VI, 1980, no.1, 1–5

Cliff Edwards, *Van Gogh and God: A Creative Spiritual Quest*, Chicago 1989

Vivian Forrester, *Van Gogh*, Amsterdam 1984

Matthew Fox, *Original Blessing; A Primer in Creation Spirituality*, Santa Fe (New Mexico) 1983

H. R. Graetz, *The Symbolic Language of Vincent van Gogh*, London 1963

A. M. Hammacher and R. Hammacher, *Van Gogh. Een documentaire biografie*, Amsterdam 1982

Hidde Hoekstra, *Rembrandt en de bijbel; het nieuwe testament.* Deel 1, *Het Kerstevangelie*; Deel 2, *Jezus van Nazareth*, Utrecht and Antwerp 1975

H. C. Honnegger, *The Religious Significance of Vincent van Gogh*

Jan Hulsker, *Lotgenoten. Het leven van Vincent en Theo van Gogh*, Weesp 1985

—, *Van Gogh in Close-up*, Amsterdam 1993

Karl Jaspers, *Strindberg und Van Gogh: Versuch einer pathographischen Analyse unter vergleichender Heranziehung von Swedenborg und Hölderlin*, Munich 1949

J. B. G. Jansen, *Barmhartige Samaritaan*, Apeldoorn 1974

Tsokasa Kodera, 'In het zweet uws aanschijns; spitters in Van Goghs oeuvre,' in *Van Gogh in Brabant*, Zwolle 1987

—, Vincent van Gogh, Christianity versus Nature (dissertation University of Amsterdam) 1988

George E. Lawrence, The Methodism of Vincent van Gogh, 1979 (unpublished thesis)

Josefine Leistra, *George Henry Boughton: God speed! Pelgrims op weg naar Canterbury*, Zwolle 1987

J. Leymarie, *Van Gogh*, Paris 1912

Sven Lövgren, *The Genesis of Modernism. Seurat, Gauguin, and French Symbolism in the 1880s*, Stockholm 1959

Somerset Maugham, *The Moon and Sixpence,* 1919 (this is a novel about Gauguin in which Van Gogh appears)

J. Meyer-Graefe, *Vincent van Gogh. Der Roman eines Gottsuchers,* Munich 1932

Jan Meyers, *De Jonge Vincent; Jaren van vervoering en vernedering,* Amsterdam 1989

R. Miedema, *Van Gogh en het evangelie,* Amsterdam 1948

Ann H. Murray, 'The Religious Background of Vincent van Gogh and its Relations to his Views on Nature and Art', *Journal of the American Academy of Religion.* XLIV 1 Supp., March 1978, 67–95

H. Nagera, *Vincent van Gogh. A Psychological Study,* London 1967

Johan P. Nater, *Vincent van Gogh: een biografie,* Rotterdam 1989

C. Nordenfalk, 'Van Gogh and Literature', *Journal of the Warburg and Courtauld Institutes* X, 1948, 132–47

Fieke Pabst, *Vincent van Gogh's Poetry Albums,* Zwolle 1958

– and Evert van Uitert, 'A Literary Life, with a List of Books and Periodicals read by Van Gogh', in E.van Uitert and M. Hoyle, *The Rijksmuseum Vincent van Gogh,* Amsterdam 1987, 68–84

R. Pickvance, English Influences on Vincent van Gogh, thesis University of Nottingham 1974–1975

Jan en Annie Romein, *Erflaters van onze beschaving,* The Hague and Antwerp 1971 (revised edition), 'Vincent van Gogh, "Meester der menselijkheid"'

Meyer Schapiro, *Vincent van Gogh,* London 1951

Susanne Scherer, Religiöse Motive im Bildwerk Vincent van Goghs, Landau 1986 (Wissenschaftliche Prüfungsarbeit)

Jean J. Sezner, 'Literary Inspiration in Van Gogh', in Bogomila Welsh Ovcharov, *Van Gogh in Perspective,* New Jersey 1974, 126–33

George Steiner, *Real Presences,* London 1989

J. Stellingwerff, *Werkelijkheid en grondmotief bij Vincent Willem van Gogh,* Amsterdam 1959

—, 'Vincent van Gogh', *Polemios* VIII, no. 11 (April 1953)

Sjuhi Takashina, 'Vincent van Gogh and French Literature', in Vincent van Gogh, *International Symposium,* Tokyo 1988, 405–17

Louis van Tilborgh, 'A Kind of Bible: The Collection of Prints and Illustrations', in E. van Uitert and M. Hoyle, *The Rijksmuseum Vincent van Gogh,* Amsterdam 1987, 38–44

—, 'Vincent van Gogh and English Social Realism', in Julian Treuherz, *Hard Times; Social Realism in Victorian Art*, London and Manchester 1987

— (ed.), *Van Gogh en Millet*, Amsterdam 1988

M. E. Tralbaut, *Vincent van Gogh in zijn Antwerpische Periode*, Amsterdam 1948

—, *Vincent van Gogh en Charles de Groux, de Kalmthoutse heide, les Japonaiseries, les femmes*, Antwerp 1953

—, 'Vincent van Gogh und die Religion', in *Van Goghiana* III, Antwerp 1966

—, *Van Gogh, le mal-aimé*, Lausanne 1969

M. E. Tralbaut, 'Over de godsdienstige richtingen in Vincents tijd', in *Van Goghiana* VII, 1970, 103–8

Evert van Uitert, 'Van Gogh, Vincents identificatie met de tot leven gewekte Lazarus', *Vrij Nederland* XXXVI, February 1975, 23

—, *Vincent van Gogh in Creative Competition*, Zutphen 1983

—, *Het geloof in de moderne kunst*, Dordrecht 1987

W. Vanbeselaere, *De hollandsche periode in het werk van Vincent van Gogh*, Antwerp and Amsterdam 1937

A. Verkade Bruining, 'Vincent's Plans to Become a Clergyman', *Vincent Bulletin* III (no.4), 1974, 14ff.; IV (no.1),1975, 9ff.

W. A. Visser 't Hooft, *Rembrandts weg tot het Evangelie*, Amsterdam 1956

Theun de Vries, *Ziet een mens* (1963), after the fourth impression it appeared under the title *Vincent in Den Haag*.

H. R. Weber, *The Laity in Ministry. Living in the Image of Christ*, Geneva 1986

M. Weisbach, *V. van Gogh, Kunst und Schicksal* (2 vols), 1949, 1950

Basil Willey, *Nineteenth-Century Studies from Coleridge to Matthew Arnold*, London 1949

I would like to express my gratitude for the help I have received from the staff of the library of the Rijksmuseum Vincent van Gogh in Amsterdam.